Know Yourself.....
Your Personality

KNOW YOURSELF.....
YOUR PERSONALITY

Satish Kumar

ISHA BOOKS
DELHI-110 033

Know Yourself .... Your Personality

(Psychology, General Reading)

Rs. 540

ISBN : 9788182051447

Published in 2015 in India by
Isha Books
D-43, Prithvi Raj Road
Delhi – 110033

Lasertype Setting by: Tact Computer Graphics, Delhi
Printed at **: Chawla Offset Press, Delhi**

Contents

A MESSAGE....

The real personality of a person lies within. The thinking makes a man strong, weak, wicked, wise, kind or bold. The thinking within crops up from many reasons, e.g. the home environment, the company and the events and experiences in life. Much depends upon the early events and experiences when one is a child or at a growing stage. Events and experinces apart, building a positive personality is within one's own hands. Knowingly or unknowingly, the parents build their own child's personality.

This book; Know Yourself...Your Personality; presents to you an awakening in the form of a story in a very easy and palatable style. This would help one improve the personality after understanding the realities of life. We need better personalities for a better future. The mind power is the will power and the development of mind is the development of personality.

The book has been written by an ex. Senior Manager; the one who has already achieved God realization through deep meditation. He has earlier written a book on mind management entitled: Human Mind, Awakening and Management.

THE TRUTH

I ASKED A FLOWER, "WHAT IS YOUR AIM?
DON'T YOUR WANT FAME?"
SAID, "I DON'T KNOW,
IN A FEW DAYS, I HAVE TO GO."

"USE ME, ABSORB ME, SOMEWHERE PUT ME,
ON YOUR FACE, A SMILE, I WANT TO SEE,
I DON'T KNOW, IF I AM WORTH FAME,
PEOPLE CALL ME BY SOME NAME."

"SOMETHING, I WANT TO ATTAIN,
MY LIFE MAY NOT GO IN VAIN,
STILL IT MAY BE SUNSHINE, IT MAY RAIN,
WITH GOD ONLY I HAVE TO REMAIN."

ONE

In a short time, he had achieved good success,
Good behaviour and smartness, he was no less,
Had a small manufacturing unit, was diligent,
His jobs used to be excellent.

He thought of always happiness,
No sadness and why sadness,
He was then of twenty-four,
Was capable of doing much more.

His father was old,
At this age, he was still bold,
Husband and wife, both had retired,
With life he never felt tired.

Money, father had enough to eat and spend,
On anyone, he did not depend,
The mother, in nature was haughty,
The command of the whole house, she felt to be her duty.

The wife was arrogant,
But, the husband, knew the art of management,
He knew when and how to criticize,
In difficult situations, his humble nature would make him rise.

The boy had one sister and one brother,
The childhood, they played together,
The brother was of nineteen,
And the sister was seventeen.

The brother was studying engineering,
Did not like much of talking,
He was a little introvert,
But, had the qualities of becoming an expert.

The parents spent a lot on his studies,
Towards parents, he knew his duties,
The mother gave him lot of love,
He felt, among everyone, she was above.

The girl was tall and lean,
Films, going here and there, she was very keen,
She was quite beautiful,
But, was not that dutiful.

Others, she did not care,
Hard work and patience, she was not aware,
She was a pampered one,
And whatever she wanted, was got done.

The father was of a religious nature,
He used to study one or the other scriptures,
The mother also used to take part in worships,
But remained more engaged in worldly matters and relationships.

She spent most of her time on phone and talks,
Or enjoyed the TV soaps,
She was involved in neighbour and home politics,
She was famous for her crude tricks.

With one she would be too good,
And with another too bad,
She would then change ends,
And followed the political trends.

Her husband never liked these tricks,
In talks he would criticize in bricks and sticks,
Nothing would deter her from this activity,
She was yet to understand properly life's reality.

****

- *LIFE IS NOT TO SPEND MEANINGLESSLY.*
- *AT THE EARLIST POSSIBLE UNDERSTAND THE REALITIES OF LIFE.*
- *TRY TO REALISE, WHAT I AM?*

****

The TV was on at full volume,
It was eight o' clock in the morning,
Nothing else was audible,
The doorbell was ringing.

The mother and the daughter, at the TV, both were concentrating,
In a closed room, the younger brother was studying,
The elder one was getting ready in his room,
The father was in the bathroom.

From the bathroom, the father heard the bell,
From there he started to yell,
The mother and the daughter, at the TV, did not hear,
In an English movie something was not getting clear.

The father came out,
Gave a little shout,
"There is someone at the door,"
She started looking at the floor.

The floor had gone a little wet,
She said, "What have you done,"
He again cried at her,
"At the door there is someone."

"You know, I am not well,"
"But, there should be someone to hear to the bell,"
He told the daughter to go,
Busy in the TV, she said, "A big NO."

In the meantime, came out the elder one,
He had given time to someone,
With anger on his face,
Towards the door he made a race.

In haste, he opened the door,
There was now no one at the door,
He turned back in a flash,
As if someone he wanted to bash.

Towards the younger sister, he made a dash,
In the house, it was the beginning of a clash,
"Why didn't you open the door?"
"Why, to do it, there are so many more."

"I don't want to listen anything,"
"Is the youngest responsible for everything?"
"In the house, what for you are responsible?
To hear, the doorbell, I think you are able."

"Morning TV, evening TV, every time TV,"
"It is not only me, everyone sees TV,"
"Not all the time,"
"Don't think it is crime."

"Did I say that?"
"You better hit me with a bat,"
"You, as if I am beating,"
"The way you are treating."

"I only want to see you more sensible,"
"To do anything, I am able,"
"Not able to hear the bell,"
"You have nothing else to tell."

"I am not telling you, without any cause,"
"For everything, you have a because,"
"An important person wanted to meet me,"
"Not me."

****

- ***IT IS THE ENVIRONMENT THAT MATTERS.***
- ***PARENTAL GUIDANCE IS MORE IMPORTANT THAN PARENTAL LOVE.***
- ***THE IRRESPONSIBLE ONE'S GATHER DUST AND NOT GOLD.***

***

The mother interrupted, "Enough is enough,"
Said the brother, "You would say, I am rough,"
"Why are you after this child?"
"She is going wild."

"She is okay. you mend yourself,"
"I can control myself,
I will have to face the loss,"
"You are yourself responsible for your loss."

"But how,"
"You were not ready on time,"
"Shortage of water, what can I do,"
"You have an excuse every time."

"Mummy, you are also not understanding me,"
"Who was he?"
"I had to work with him on a tender,"
"You should have been on time, you are not tender."

"You mean there is no one else to open the door here,"
"You take care of your own work, is that clear,"
"I am taking care of my work, mummy,"
"Everyone else is dummy."

Father spoke in between, "You have talked enough, stop now,"
The mother said, "Do you think I am a cow,"
"I have never stopped you to speak,"
"Don't think I am weak."

"I am not saying that, you should take care of the house,
On TV you are just watching cat and mouse,"
"I know what is important,
I am not house's attendant."

"Opening the door, no one becomes an attendant,
It is a question of only temperament,"
"All this talk, many times, I have heard,
All absurd."

"I know you are sensible enough,
You unnecessarily get rough,"
"I know what is to be done for the house,
And I was not watching mouse."

"I am also not speaking nonsense,
This is all your arrogance,"
"Don't make me more tense,
Otherwise, I will teach all of you proper sense."

"You have been teaching me sense all these years,
It is me only who bears,"
"Because what I say is correct,
I know I am perfect."

"Life is not all to be spent like this,
Kitty parties, phones, cards, and all that rubbish,"
"You mean, I should lock myself in a room,
And think of the doom."

"Everything is good up to a certain limit,
Spending all your time like this, sense does not permit,"
"I know how to spend time,
I am not doing any crime."

"Life is not only, like this, to enjoy,
We are aged now, not girl or boy,"
"The matter was of opening the door,
I don't want to hear your lecture any more."

****

- ***MOTHER CAN PLAY A GREAT ROLE IN SHAPING A CHILD.***
- ***IF THE ELDER'S MIND IS NOT UNDER CONTROL, WHAT ABOUT THE YOUNGSTERS?***
- ***PARENT'S IRRESPONSIBLE BEHAVIOUR WOULD INCULCATE***
- ***IRRESPONSIBILITY ALONE AMONG THE CHILDREN.***

****

"Right now, I am talking about your attitude,
Your lifestyle has made you only rude,"
"That is my style,
No one can stand before me for a while."

"What to talk of the knowledge within,
At least, you could have gained knowledge from books,"
"Don't talk about my knowledge,
I can make people hang on the hooks."

"Hanging people on the hooks, don't make you great,
It depends upon your understanding about humanity and the environment you create,"
"As if I have created a hell,
Only by not listening to the bell."

"I am not talking about the bell, I am talking about your understanding about life,
Life is not to use your tongue like a knife,"
"If you cannot use your tongue properly,
You cannot call my tongue unruly."

"Now is the time, we should devote more in meditation,
For us that is the best recreation,"
"Might be correct,
Why not have this sort of recreation."

"An act, which you do,
Should not have a negative effect on others,"
"It should have a positive effect on me,
Who cares about others?"

- ***WE HAVE COME ON THIS EARTH TO,
LIVE WITH OTHERS,
ADJUST WITH OTHERS,
LOVE OTHERS,
RESPECT OTHERS,
GUIDE OTHERS,
AND HELP OTHERS,
BUT, NOT HURT OTHERS.***
- ***THE UNDERSTANDING ABOUT LIFE
INCREASES MORE AND MORE,
AS WE MEDITATE ON HIM REGULARLY.***

TWO

The father went away,
Thinking he cannot, any longer, stay,
The lady felt victorious,
For such acts she was notorious.

A small incident changed the scene,
Outside, it was all- serene,
Inside, the minds were filled with rage,
The bodies were at a boiling stage.

The scene would have been different totally,
Had they thought and dealt with the situation wisely,
Words spoken in anger and haste,
May, in seconds, spoil the entire joyful taste.

The lady wanted to remain the strongest,
Did not care for the feelings of the rest,
She wanted to remain the most important,
This desire had a great impact on her temperament.

The elder son was tense,
He could not do much in this situation,
He left for the office,
For the mother and the daughter continued, the recreation.

The old man got lost in prayers,
His mood, he took some time to repair,
Got lost in meditation,
And soon forgot the morning affair.

He left the quarrel in between,
Someone may consider it his weakness,
But it was his internal greatness,
It was because of his inner calmness.

Had he not left, in between, that quarrel,
The house may still have been in a whirl,
If one person can damage the whole condition,
The other can control the whole situation.

The lady went to a party,
The girl was busy on phone,
With a daughter and son at home,
The father was feeling somewhat alone.

He looked out of the house,
Some children were playing,
The mind got diverted,
He saw in his thoughts, some kids smiling and walking.

He thought of his own son,
And then he thought of his son's son,
He had settled,
And could now get married.

He thought of, how he cried,
How he played,
How he studied,
But, again got disturbed.

By marring a son,
Could all the happiness be won?
One truth, one doesn't get all the wishes,
Wishes don't die; the man perishes.

As he was thinking of the happiness, ahead,
Seeing his son getting wed,
The telephone bell rang,
"I would come by evening", told the wife with a bang.

*****

- ***THE INNER STRENGTH IS MORE IMPORTANT THAN EXTERNAL.***
- ***IF YOU FEEL PEACE IS GOLD, KEEP YOUR NERVES UNDER CONTROL.***
- ***THE REAL PEACE EMANATES FROM WITHIN.***

*****

Everyone was at home by nine,
They collected together to dine,
Everyone got involved in the food,
The scene showed the house's sick Mood.

The mother was rather sad,
Her mood was quite bad,
Someone outside cheated her and she wanted to sue,
This angry mood, for the house was not new.

The father talked about the son's wedding,
But, the mother, after an angry day talked about bedding,
The marriage talk could not get much headway,
And it was called a day.

The elder son, in the day could reconcile a little,
But, he knew that the life is a battle,
With difficulties he was prepared to fight till the end,
And not to get nervous; at any bend.

The father was watching the stars,
And was thinking of the behavioural wars,
He was thinking of wars within,
And of the wars outside.

What makes a man fight?
It was dead silence at night,
Suddenly, two cats started to fight,
And spoiled the silence of the night.

—

What about mind's silence?
Why it gets into violence?
Mind or God, what works,
No, not God, it is the mind that works.

Next morning, the father again opened the topic of son's marriage,
The mother was busy in make up,
The sons and daughter were busy somewhere,
The marriage talk again did not come up.

On this issue, the son was tight-lipped,
By the father, this silence was noticed,
The father tried to ask him,
But, he avoided and said, "I am going to gym."

The silence was difficult to bear,
And nothing was clear,
There is silence that provides peace,
But, a silence creates unease.

After two days, the mother spoke,
There is a girl, my friend's daughter,
Everyone heard it,
A single word, the boy, did not utter.

This silence was noticed by the mother,
The matter was discussed by the mother and father together,
He was asked his views, to marry,
A peaceful answer was, "I have my business to carry."

The mother stressed to answer properly,
And to answer, negatively or positively,
But, the question hanged on,
And he told the mother to answer later on.

After a few days, the mother and father again questioned,
For half an hour, he was grilled and detained,
He; then came out with the truth,
It was a problem common to youth.

*****

- **SILENCE IS A WEAPON OF THE STRONG.**
- **IT IS DIFFICULT TO WIN THE INNER FIGHT AND TO KEEP THE TONGUE UNDER CONTROL.**
- **THE REAL TEST LIES IN KEEPING CALM AND WINNING THE GAME.**

*****

He said, "I don't want girl's list,"
"I am in love with my receptionist,"
She was beautiful, but from a different state,
The news, a problem, it did create.

The mother got furious,
For that matter she was very religious,
"You dare not speak about that girl,"
And a few abuses, she did hurl.

In the house, this was the beginning of a fresh quarrel,
The father did not take part in this battle,
The boy was in a whirl,
The father in a corner was thinking a little.

As the discussion moved up and down,
The faces turned red and brown,
Once again, the house's peace was broken,
In the mother's mind, a serious storm did awaken.

The son gave his arguments out,
From his angle, he had no doubt,
The mother's rage was too strong,
She held the son absolutely wrong.

The son was adamant,
The mother was adamant,
It was a big crisis,
Whose mistake it was her or his?

The other girl, the son was not ready to accept,
It was difficult to reach a decision,
The mother tried a lot,
But, he was not prepared to listen to any suggestion.

Crisis management is also an art,
It requires a strong head and heart,
It is not at all required to make a noise,
What is required is to have poise.

The father thought and thought,
These names who has brought,
A man, by birth is only a man,
A man labels by caste and creed another man.

The God does not come in between all this,
The mistake is not His,
The man créates differences,
Using his mind and senses.

It is true that the living style may not be liked by each other,
But, with time they can change and adjust their styles and come together,
First, for the change, they should agree,
Then, the change can be effected to any degree.

The main problem is that, to change, man does not agree,
They agree to disagree,
To reach agreements is within man's hand,
The difficult part is to change the stand.

Change is part of life's game,
Things never remain the same,
One who cannot go with others,
On the way only hate he gathers.

There was once again a silence on the matter,
The father started the talk,
The mother looked up in anger,
The son on hearing, got up and started to walk.

*****

- ***EMOTIONAL ADJUSTMENTS IN LIFE IS A MUST IN TESTING SITUATIONS.***
- ***ADJUSTMENTS GIVE RELIEF.***
- ***IT REQUIRES A MINDSET TO ADJUST.***

*****

The father, caught the son by his arm and smiled,
By then, the father had reconciled,
The son looked at the serious mother,
And then the smiling father.

To break the silence, he was not in a mood,
Emotionless, he just stood,
He was afraid of mother's rudeness,
And of her thinking crudeness.

Father's face, he could read,
He had, by now, agreed,
Mother's face was red hot,
He remembered the warning he got.

The mother had told, to just forget her,
"The matter is closed,
If you do not leave her,
This door, for you, may be closed."

The son had thought of roses,
Not of abuses,
The father's hand was giving him a little strength,
Wanted to talk at length.

How to control the mother,
Perhaps, father and myself can tackle together,
"What about marriage, my son," he spoke,
The silence, he broke.

"He would marry my friend's daughter,
That other girl is not allowed even to drink this house's water,
I cannot have that relation,
Even by looking at her, I get some irritation."

The son said softly, "But have you some idea about her thoughts,
The way she talks,
And what is wrong in her appearance,
And that temperance."

The mother said strongly, "You better shut up,
With you, I am really fed up,
When I say something, that has to be accepted,
That girl stands rejected."

"You think of my friend,
You think of that family,
You think of their status,
And don't be so silly."

"I am silly only,
I don't want to talk,
Only Dad wanted to talk,
I knew the house would just start to rock."

The father said, "You better control your angry tone,
In this marriage, I don't see anything wrong,
Such marriages are talking place,
She is a good girl, to whatever religion she may belong."

"In our house, we can make the girl adjust,
Please don't unnecessarily resist,
Let us be realistic,
And not egotistic."

"Rather than hurling harsh words at each other,
Let us try to understand each other,
We should try to solve the problem by discussing,
Rather than abusing."

*****

- ***THE SOUL WITHIN IS SIMILAR; IT HAS NO COLOR, CASTE OR CREED.***
- ***ONLY THE BODIES ARE DIFFERENT, THE MINDS ARE DIFFERENT.***
- ***THE SOUL IS AN IMMACULATE PART OF GOD.***

*****

The father continued, "Harshness can only create more differences,
The mind doesn't forget those utterances,
Mind works properly, when one is cool,
Don't let the anger rule."

"The boy is not immature,
Any problem, he can find a cure,
Our behaviour should be soft,
A better language we should adopt."

"I know my language,
I am also of a mature age,
I am not going to change my mind,
Nothing of that kind."

At this the father got a little angry,
And told her to go away,
"I will take the decision,
Let me see who comes in my way."

Father, although soft, knew the way to be hard,
He, very rarely, used this card,
He still told her to think about it logically,
And just don't frown angrily.

Days passed, the boy did not change the stand,
The father stood firmly by his stand,
The mother was silent on this affair,
There was an uneasy calm in the air.

The faces of the three could easily suggest,
That their minds were not at rest,
The peace of the home was lost somewhere,
Why so, are they all aware?

The son wants to find peace in his love,
The father in the son's love,
Is the mother trying to find peace somewhere?
Yes, in her superiority complex, in the whole affair.

This feeling was difficult to overcome,
She was struggling within,
The father could see this struggle,
Simply, she wanted to win.

The father tried to assuage the anger,
The mother, to talk on the subject, was not eager,
She would not say yes or no,
What to do, the boy did not know.

The family members used to meet at TV or dining table,
They used to talk in different directions,
They would laugh and smile also,
They would talk of their other relations.

On the marriage issue, there were no talks,
All had taken their stand like rocks,
The boy now wanted to discuss,
For him, it was a long recess.

The boy and the girl often used to meet outside,
The wishes of the mother and father, he wanted to abide,
Friendship, he could not break,
Perhaps, some adjustments he was trying to make.

When he talked to his friends,
They suggested marrying without parent's permission,
He was mature enough,
And never accepted this suggestion.

*****

- ***TREAT YOUR YOUNG CHILD AS YOUR STUDENT AND MATURE SON OR DAUGHTER AS YOUR FRIEND.***
- ***ONE HAS TO GIVE LOVE AND RESPECT TO GET LOVE AND RESPECT.***
- ***RUDENESS GATHERS SADNESS ALONE.***

*****

The father wanted the mother to agree,
As he did not want to divide the house in two parts,
He could force the marriage,
But, he knew, it would be difficult to heal the cuts.

He hoped that things would change,
His views with anyone, he could not exchange,
He wanted to talk to the boy,
But, he knew, as of now, he could not get him joy.

The, mother sometimes, might be thinking on these lines,
But, her mind remained busy with friends, playing cards, tens and nines,
She used to remain very less at home,
And used to talk more with friends about UK and ROME.

Perhaps, she was thinking that the boy would one day bow,
Perhaps, his feeling she did not properly assess and know,
She considered her son shy and meek,
But meek should not be considered weak.

In home affairs, she took less interest,
She did not know to what extent his son could resist,
It is not that one should not enjoy with friends,
But, it depends from person to person, how the home affairs one attends.

The mind might be busy in many places,
The mind might be engaged in many races,
The mind might be engrossed in many arenas,
But, the mind should not forget the priority areas.

The mother considered herself to be the leader,
But, did not have the qualities of a leader,
Important marriage issue, she was not prepared to discuss,
The magnitude of the problem, she did not assess.

More than a year had passed, the matter hanged in a confused state,
In such a time, the paths can deviate,
In case of love tangles,
One should consider all angles.

The father tried a lot,
But priority to this job, she could not allot,
The father tried to talk to the boy indirectly,
The boy never opened up exactly.

The father tried to persuade,
But, the love question he would always evade,
The love problem in this situation is difficult to solve,
Specially, when the boy and girl have taken a strong resolve.

The real love has to be sincere-spirited,
Should not be short-lived,
Should not change into hatred,
And should be at a mature age, wisely decided.

Should not be a blind love,
Should not be greed filled love,
Should not be based only on attractions,
Should consider all reactions and ramifications.

The boy was now getting impatient,
No one, except the father considered the matter as important,
He was now thinking of marrying without parent's permission,
He was now thinking to fall in with friend's suggestion.

The mother's silence,
Coupled with her arrogance,
Was now forcing the boy to do,
Which he did not want to do.

*****

- ***STUBBORN MINDS ENJOY AT THE COST OF OTHERS FEELINGS.***
- ***DISHARMONY CAN CAUSE SERIOUS INJURIES.***
- ***WHEN THE MIND FLIES HIGH, ONE FORGETS IN THE ENJOYMENT OF THE***
- ***FLIGHT, THE REACTION TO SOME OF HIS ACTIONS.***

*****

The boy till now, soft and simple,
To do anything, he was capable,
Was now going to take a wrong step,
Its responsibility, who would accept.

Are the parents wrong?
Is the boy wrong?
The mother is bound by her mind,
And the son by his mind.

The boy talked to the girl,
He proposed to marry her in a temple,
The girl first disagreed,
It was a task not so simple.

The girl had been brought up by the mother,
Because of the early death of the father,
The mother was aged,
She was, however, not moneyed.

The girl's mother was soft-spoken and well mannered,
The whole life she had worked,
Her whole life was a struggle,
Her only daughter, she now wanted to settle.

The girl was fully trained and taught,
She knew to remain within limits,
She would not take any wrong step,
She knew the repercussions of crossing the limits.

She knew the meaning of the womanhood,
She knew the meaning of the motherhood,
She could not be easily taken in,
She knew the art to win.

The real personality of a person lies in his thinking process within,
It is the thinking that makes him or her strong and patient within,
The appearances can be misleading,
The real test lies in knowing one's thinking.

The girl narrated the facts to her mother,
She somewhat knew about their friendship,
She raised several questions,
And then started thinking deeply, if they could have this relationship.

Mother's past was very unpleasant,
She never wanted to take a decision, which later has to repent,
She thought and thought, but herself, she could not convince,
But then she thought, the boy was no less than a prince.

They can marry on their own,
But, what will be the boy's mother's reaction,
Will she own them or disown?
Why not, in advance take some action.

Why not talk to the boy's parents,
After all they are human beings,
The boy and girl are mature enough to decide,
Why should we stop, living together, these two beings?

They may insult me,
They may refuse,
But marrying the children without talking to them,
Later on, to face the society, we will have no excuse.

The girl's mother tried to talk to boy's parents on phone,
The boy's mother refused to talk,
The boy's father was not at home,
She was told, some other door she may knock.

*****

- *A CAREFULLY CONSIDERED LOVE IS ALSO LOVE. GOD HAS GIVEN US BOTH THE MIND AND THE BODY TO MAKE LOVE. IF THE MIND HAS THE LOVING CAPABILITY, IT HAS THE WISE THINKING ABILITY ALSO.*
- *THE WISE THINKING ABILITY INCREASES WITH MEDITATION AND SPEAKING OF MANTRAS, LIKE THE GAYATRI MANTRA.*
- *THE DICTATES OF THE MIND SHOULD NOT BE TAKEN, AS DESTINY. EVERYONE IS RESPONSIBLE FOR HIS DEEDS.*

*****

Both the boy and the girl were mature,
About their loyalties, they were quite sure,
With a heavy heart, the mother allowed them to marry,
Always thinking, later on, she may not have to feel sorry.

The boy's mother could never expect her son to marry without permission,
She was not prepared for such a situation,
The son thought of father's love and respect,
But, then he thought, later on, he would tackle this aspect.

My father would be sad to know about my action,
But I would see the happiness in his reaction,
Mother, I don't know,
I will, after marriage, better bow.

For the marriage, a time and date was fixed,
Happiness, worry, uneasiness all got mixed,
The girl's mother was present at the wedding,
But, was it a marriage ceremony with a happy ending?

Who is responsible for all this?
Who is responsible for reducing marriage's happiness?
Is it destiny?
Or mind's ordered deeds?

The boy's mother and father were unaware,
The boy was getting wed somewhere,
The mother could have solved the affair,
But, could not cross that superiority layer.

Only the mind is the culprit,
Its flight, one needs to edit,
Later on, against God you may issue a writ,
Yelling it's His mistake, and He should admit.

But, will He admit?
He would say, "Fates I don't knit,
Fate, you can't lend or borrow,
Your own bad deeds, this birth or previous births bring sorrow."

THREE

The ceremony of the marriage at the temple was now complete,
Marrying without parents, written in their minds, they could not delete,
Now was the time to face them,
Now was the time to take blessing from them.

The girl's mother was also in a state of great doubt,
But, in God she had great faith, beyond doubt,
The boy and the girl, at home, pressed the bell,
Praying to God, that everything should go well.

Boy's sister came out, seeing, suddenly went back,
Then came the boy's mother to get a severe attack,
"So, you got married,"
In an angry tone, she cried.

"We are sorry mummy,"
"Don't call me mummy,"
As the son went near,
She went back, saying, "Why have you come here?"

"What have you done?
Before all this, why didn't you kill me with a gun?
What would people say?
They would think that I am only a dummy made of clay."

"I will not accept,
Anyone else may call it correct,
How dare you do such an act?
Your mother, how could you neglect."

"I think she is responsible for it,
This net she did knit,
You don't know whom did you hit,
I will see to it."

In the meantime, came the father, shocked for a while,
Then, came out a small smile,
The boy and the girl had a sigh of relief,
But, the father's smile was very brief.

He came out sternly, "What is this?
You should not have taken a step like this,
All this doesn't look nice,
I don't know, who gave you this advice."

"I think I did not properly educate,
Or is it our fate,
Isn't it a hit on our own happiness?
I think we are ourselves responsible for this mess."

"Had, earlier, we accepted,
This situation would not have erupted,
You did not think of family's prestige,
I don't know who gave you so much of courage."

"But, I as His true man, accept this marriage,
No one can stop, you both are of marriageable age,"
Told his wife to put the rage in a cage,
"As for rage, this is not the proper stage."

The mother cried,
"Why have I not yet died?
You may accept,
I have rejected and I again reject."

"Let them stay here,
As they can't go elsewhere,
But, they can't find me happy,
I am not a baby."

*****

- ***WISDOM LIES IN RECOVERING FROM AWKWARD SITUATIONS AS QUICKLY AS POSSIBLE.***
- ***WISDOM LIES IN ADJUSTING ONESELF AS PER THE CIRCUMSTANCES.***
- ***WHEN THE MIND MERGES WITH THE SOUL AND CONSULTS THE SOUL BEFORE TAKING AN ACTION, SUCH ACTION CAN BE CONSIDERED AS EQUIVALENT TO GOD'S ACTION.***

*****

The situation somewhat got settled,
For a long, by now, they had battled,
The new member had now entered,
Attention on a reception was now being centered.

For the girl, it was a testing situation,
With everyone she had to develop a new relation,
She wanted to win the mother-in-law,
But, was afraid to get into her claw.

The father arranged a good reception,
Many friends and relatives attended the celebration,
There were smiles and many danced,
There were many with eyebrows raised.

There were talks in the mid,
"What this boy did?"
"He could have a better girl,"
"Perhaps, he got into some whirl."

The boy's mother sat in a corner, with her sisters,
Talks were going on in whispers,
She looked very grim,
As if something was boiling to the brim.

She was feeling insulted,
She was disgusted,
The girl, she hated,
And thought the entire problem for her, she has created.

She was not seen smiling for a while,
It was too difficult for her to reconcile,
Had she earlier thought and spoken,
Perhaps, this situation would not have arisen.

Is she not herself responsible for her own condition?
Has she not trapped herself in this situation?
In such situations, if one doesn't control his mind,
Wrath would further make him blind.

Came the guests, who spoke against,
Her anger, she could not resist,
In one corner was the father, filled with delight,
In another was his wife, feeling jealous at that sight.

The guests who spoke negatively,
Added fuel to the fire,
Is it fair on their part,
To add to someone's ire.

The father wanted everyone to live in harmony,
He wanted all to live together happily,
Everyone should adjust and cooperate now,
He was thinking all positively.

The thinking of all in the house has to be positive,
Everyone in nature should be supportive,
The warmth of love can help face many awkward situations,
But, hatred can destroy all solutions.

The situation in their house was problematic,
It needed care,
The father counseled his wife,
And suggested her to be fair.

The mother agreed and nodded,
The father was quite satisfied,
All care was being taken of the newly wed,
The couple was happy, the way the father, their family he had led.

*****

- ***MAN IS HIMSELF RESPONSIBLE FOR HIS SORROWS.***
- ***ILL-TREATING SOMEONE MEANS GOING AGAINST THE NATURE, AS YOU, ME, HE OR SHE ARE ALL PARTS OF NATURE.***
- ***THE BEST MIND PURIFIER IS YOUR OWN SOUL.***

*****

The couple went for honeymooning,
It was raining and snowing,
They enjoyed a lot,
It can't be measured, the happiness they got.

They forgot all that unpleasant past,
Hours and days just flew very fast,
Now was the time to go back,
Marriage puts a girl on a totally new track.

The girl, in nature, was soft and not at all rough,
To face the problems, within she was tough,
But, she was not used to rough language,
She felt better, if there was someone to encourage.

She could adjust with everyone,
She had malice towards none,
She was prepared to accept any style of worship,
She knew such adjustments, would be required for
the smooth sailing of life's ship.

The only fear she had, she was of a different caste,
Some problems it may cast,
Others feelings, she would respect,
A good treatment, she did expect.

She knew the situation was delicate,
It could flare up with any mistake,
A sweet home she wanted to make,
Any wrong step, not to take.

What is planned is sometimes achieved and sometimes not,
But planning has to be done,
Planning anything is of a great importance,
Mostly, with proper planning, people have won.

Planning is mind's job,
Something else may come on the way,
Man has to do his job,
Let the nature have its say.

Thoughts, thoughts and thoughts and came the home,
She had now started thinking her own,
A girl when enters the husband's house, thinks everything her own,
She thinks, her husband is her own and everything connected with him her own.

It is for the husband to rise to her faith,
To give her love and the desired respect,
It is for the entire family to look after the new member,
And to take care of her every need and not to neglect.

The girl has to extend respect,
Otherwise, the desired respect, she may not attract,
There is one important aspect,
When irritation and anger comes on the way, that time is one's real test.

It was early in the morning,
The birds were chirping,
In the veranda, the newly wed were sitting,
The air was singing.

Came out the boy's mother,
She had a serious face,
The girl said with a smile, "Good morning, mummy,"
There was no reply, but anger on the face did surface.

"Don't you know, the daughter-in-law has to touch the feet and bow?
This shows respect,
Your mother did not tell you,
Such an important aspect."

*****

- ***CAN RESPECT BE FORCED BY MAKING SOMEONE BOW?***
- ***THE REAL RESPECT LIES IN ONE'S MIND. THE FACE AND EYES SPEAK OF IT.***
- ***BOW WITH REAL RESPECT IN YOUR MIND.***

*****

"I am sorry mummy," and she bowed,
"I didn't know,
Please tell me what jobs I have to do,
I shall do and then to the office, I would go."

"You go to office,
Any job here, you need not do,
You attend to office,
Jobs, I will do."

In the office she was now a boss,
At the office, a warm welcome she received,
She felt elated,
At a small party, she was respected.

The boy got a helping hand,
They decided to work hand in hand,
She started to learn to work as a boss,
By marrying, she did feel she was, nowhere at a loss.

But the atmosphere at the home was mysterious,
Sometimes, it looked to be rather serious,
At home, she used to do some jobs,
But was told not to do kitchen jobs.

About this, she could not understand much,
She was lost in husband's love, and was not as such worried,
At office, she got very busy,
She noticed at certain talks and decisions, at home, she was barred.

Whenever she saw mother and daughter sitting and laughing,
She would go towards them; they stopped talking,
She was now feeling ignored,
Her doubts soared.

Perhaps, I didn't bring dowry,
At this, sometimes, she felt really sorry,
Perhaps, they don't like me,
What can I do, to make them like me?

Nights and days passed,
She was being treated as an outsider,
Except the father and husband, no one talked with her properly,
Living in a family, she was feeling herself a stranger.

One day, in the morning, she went to the kitchen to make tea,
Soon, came the mother-in-law and told her to leave,
"I will get you tea in your room,
You are daily getting it there, I believe."

She went back to her room, shaken,
She felt very bad,
She didn't tell this to her husband,
But, remained quite sad.

She was in the habit of forgetting such things quickly,
She was not in the habit of thinking negatively,
She thought, one day the relations would improve,
My marriage, she would approve.

In the office, she had learned her job completely,
While at office, office jobs absorbed her thoughts totally,
The husband and wife, many times in the evenings went out,
Roamed, but about the mother-in-law she never talked about.

One day when she was at home,
Came the mother-in-law's friends,
She wished in a respectful manner,
There was no response from any of the friends.

*****

- ***PATIENCE PAYS IN LIFE.***
- ***CONTROL ON EMOTIONS IS THE FIRST STEP TOWARDS A PATIENT ATTITUDE.***
- ***USE THE MIND'S ANALYTICAL POWER TO HAVE CONTROL ON EMOTIONS.***

*****

Asked one of the friends, "Who is she?"
Something in her ear, the mother-in-law whispered,
The lady then turned,
After that at her, only she stared.

It was very much insulting,
As if, stones of hatred she was pelting,
But the girl didn't weep,
In a sad mood, in her room she went to sleep.

The boy could notice the marks of agony on her face,
The signs of sadness,
The usual smile was missing,
As if she was suffering from some illness.

He could not resist and asked,
"What is the matter?
You don't look to be okay,
What is the problem? Why don't you utter?"

She moved her head negatively,
And moved from that place silently,
Once she thought, she may tell,
But upon knowing, the mother-in-law may create a hell.

It would disturb our peace of mind,
Some other way let me find,
Let me talk something else,
Let me take my mind somewhere else.

She started to smile,
The husband suspected for a little while,
Then got lost in talks and other things,
The time flew on wings.

Perhaps, the mother-in-law wanted her to react,
But wisely she did act,
Perhaps, the mother-in-law meant some harm,
Silently, one can show one's strong arm.

The girl had in mind the hidden feeling about dowry and caste,
She wanted somehow to bring in harmony, fast,
But things were moving in other direction,
What could be mother-in-law's expectation?

The girl thought to present her a gift,
In her action, she was very swift,
From the market, a sari she bought,
Let me gift it on her birthday, she thought.

Came the birthday,
It was early morning,
As she saw her mother-in-law,
Presented the sari with a good morning.

She didn't say thank you,
Said the girl, " It is birthday gift for you,"
"So you want to bribe me,
Whose plan, who is he?"

"It is not a bribe,
It is out of love and respect, what else should I describe,
I have purchased it out of my own,
To anyone else, it is not even known."

"So you wanted to see how I would react,
Do you think I would accept?
Saris, I have too many,
This sari, don't be so funny."

*****

- *DIVERSION OF MIND IS NECESSARY TO GET OUT OF SADNESS AND WORRY.*
- *MEDITATION HELPS A LOT DIVERT ONE'S MIND.*
- *THE ABILITY TO CONTROL EMOTIONS HELPS YOU SUCCEED IN LIFE.*

*****

"Please accept it, you are so good,
Please forget the past,
Don't treat me like this,
Disrespect to you, I can't think till the last."

"I have refused it, and that is all,
And don't try to flatter,"
Hearing something, came out the father and son,
And asked about the matter.

Said the son, "Whose sari it is?"
"It is a birthday gift for mummy,"
"That is great,
Happy birthday to you, mummy."

"Mummy, please accept it,
Mummy, Why don't you accept it?"
"With her you have also joined,
So both of you had planned."

"Mummy, she is your well-wisher,
About the sari, I didn't know or hear,
This is presented to you with sincere affection,
With you, she wants to have a good relation."

"I don't want any present,
Let me go, many jobs I have to attend,
This sari, she can wear,
Sincere affection, please don't pretend."

Said the father, "What you are doing is not good,
In accepting a sari, what is wrong?
Embrace the children,
You will not accept them, for how long."

"I know what to do,
I don't require anyone's advice,
I am not accepting the present,
In that, I am not committing any vice."

"Don't be so rude,
Soften your attitude,
This is the time for the children to enjoy,
Like this, don't reduce their joy."

"We are all human beings,
We can commit mistakes,
But, there is an end to everything,
Let us now bury all the hates."

"Let us land into finer mornings,
Let us forget the past happenings,
Let us sit and laugh together,
The dust of the past, let us not gather."

Without speaking a word, the mother-in-law went inside,
With sari in her hand, the daughter-in-law remained outside,
Sullen faces, dried lips, no smiles,
Odd and sad appearances.

No happiness, on the happy birthday,
Self knitted unhappiness with the sun's first ray,
The key to happiness lies in one's own hands,
It depends, the way, life one understands.

Thought the father, why she acted like this!
What her intention is!
She should have weighed the effect of her action,
She should have thought of the reaction.

*****

- ***WHEN ONE IS ON THE PRIDE'S RIDE, WRONG ACTIONS GENERALLY APPEAR TO BE RIGHT.***
- ***ANGER BREEDS ANGER AND UNREST.***
- ***IF WE DON'T BURY THE UNPLEASANT PAST AND REMAIN WHIRLED IN THE WAVES OF THE PAST, WE WOULD LOSE OUR FUTURE TOO.***

*****

The birthday passed off without a sparkle,
At night the dinner was as usual,
Everyone was busy eating,
Even the eyes were not meeting.

There was seriousness on daughter-in-law's face,
Still, she didn't lose grace,
With her husband, she was quite fine,
But, her husband didn't feel that fine.

On his mind, the incident left a scar,
Within, he was at war,
The morning incident, he could not forget,
At times he felt that the wife's eyes were wet.

But then he thought, the wounds, the time would heal,
Her hatred, time would steal,
It is better to remain silent,
Instead of becoming violent.

When I was going for a walk,
I heard two birds talk,
"When men come on the road,
On the nature, they create a big load."

"Why so,"
"Don't you know?"
"Yes, they create pollution,
For that there is no solution."

"Their minds are also polluted,
Their peace, this has diluted,"
"Just watch them for a while,
That supercilious smile."

"I would never like to become a man,
On their birth we should put a ban,"
"Why they think themselves so superior,"
"They live on pride filled air."

FOUR

Everyone got busy in his or her task,
What other one was doing, no one would ask,
Mother-in-law's daughter was now in the college,
She was nineteen years of age.

The mother had given her a lot of freedom,
She was allowed to have boy friends,
Any type of dress, she was allowed to wear,
The freedom given to her was now crossing certain ends.

As the son came to know of it,
He objected to it,
The father also objected,
But all such talks, the mother rejected.

One day she would go with one boy,
The other day, with another boy,
As per her, the life was to enjoy,
She enjoyed as per her definition of joy.

The mother would say, "This is the latest trend,
What is bad in having a friend?
She knows the limits,
And she would not cross the limits."

The father would say, "Let it be today's trend,
But it can have a terrible end,"
The girl was very near to the mother,
And both enjoyed together.

Her behaviour at home was very rude,
She considered herself very shrewd,
With her bhabi she was having very poor relations,
She would try to put her in awkward situations.

A girl of this age should have the knowledge of the world,
This role to impart knowledge, generally a mother plays,
She can have knowledge from the books,
A mistake at this stage can be the beginning of her bad days.

The flight of the mind, there is a need to control,
This flying bird plays a great role,
An analysis of the right and the wrong can be of great use in this way,
Proper guidance can help boys and girls not going astray.

She should have the power to assess,
Should take prudent decisions,
Should be based on the intellect,
She should know the real meaning of boy and girl relations.

Wrong judgement and decisions can play havoc,
No coming back,
Repentance does not pay,
Later on, you may call it fate or nature's attack.

Nature's attack is the one that can't be avoided,
But certain deeds can certainly be avoided,
Ill feelings, the man first nurses,
The God, later on he curses.

The girl's friends had similar thinking,
Their parents allowed late nightclubs and even drinking,
The company matters a lot,
Can make, break or destroy whatever you have got.

All the girls had boy friends and some special friends,
The girl, with a boy, got into a deep involvement,
She didn't know much about the boy,
But, with him she had developed a deep attachment.

*****

- ***BEFORE TAKING A DECISION, TRY TO ENVISAGE.***
- ***CHOOSE YOUR COMPANY WITH PRUDENCE.***
- ***TRY TO SHOW OTHERS THE RIGHT PATH, INSTEAD OF YOURSELF GOING ASTRAY.***

*****

Where this deep attachment would take her, she did not know much,
But, for a good partner, she was in search,
On her, worked no advice,
She didn't want to understand what is virtue or vice.

Those who waste and lose their youth,
Have to repent after realizing the truth,
No doubt, youth is a golden time to enjoy,
But, in this period, most of the life's gold one has to buy.

At one stage, the gold is education,
At another, it is recreation,
It can be life's settlement,
It can be life's attainment.

Attainment is more important than recreation,
Attainment brings in mind's jubilation,
Attainment is an asset,
Youth is the time to attain, and not to neglect.

The mother didn't know about girl's attachment,
It was all in name of enjoyment,
After clearing first year, she told the mother the whole affair,
She told that she couldn't live without him and he also takes her care.

The mother got annoyed,
But, didn't tell it to anyone,
First, she wanted to know about the boy,
She started the enquiry through someone.

She came to know that the boy was a great flirt,
He belonged to a rich family,
He had earlier roamed with many girls,
She was told that to think about this boy was silly.

This news put the mother in deep thoughts,
Perhaps, I had given her a long rope,
Thinking that she would behave properly,
But, she went against my hope.

She didn't know, what to do now,
The girl, she scolded,
But the girl was firm,
But, to such a boy how could she be related.

The mother was now repenting,
Any way out she was not getting,
Like the mother, the girl was adamant,
She still thought that her choice was excellent.

The girl and the mother were engaged in serious discussions,
This was noticed by the father and the son,
The father asked, what the matter was?
Looking at the sister's face, the brother asked, "What has she done?"

"She has found a boy for herself," said the mother,
But didn't tell all the facts,
She was now feeling ashamed,
Somewhat sorry for her earlier acts.

Said the brother, "Who is the boy?"
"The boy is very rich,"
"What is the boy doing?"
"He is studying."

"Is the boy rich or father rich?"
"They are rich,"
"Where he lives?"
"How does it matter, wherever he lives?"

*****

- ***YOUR ENJOYMENTS MAY NOT TURN OUT TO BE A NIGHTMARE.***
- ***UNDERSTAND LIFE FULLY AND THEN TAKE DECISIONS REGARDING LOVE AND MARRIAGE.***
- ***EMOTIONAL JUDGEMENTS CAN BE DANGEROUS.***

*****

"What more you know about the boy?"
"I know he is a moneyed and handsome boy,"
"How do you know, he is moneyed?"
"Do you think, he has lied?"

"So, you think boys don't lie,"
"He has promised, for me, he can die,"
"Let us hope that he is not a liar,"
"Do you think that that big car he has taken on hire?"

Said the father, "At the earliest, this boy, let us meet,
She doesn't understand the seriousness of this relation,
You are still a kid,
Who gave you the permission to make such a selection?"

Facing the mother, the girl said, "I am not the only one,
A boy, every girl is selecting,
What have I done?
And how are you treating."

Said the father, "There is a proper age and time for everything,
The relationship and love which you are talking is a very delicate string,
What you are talking is not at all correct,
You should have taken help of your parents, for the boy, to select."

The father said to the mother, "When did you come to know?
Isn't the matter serious?
What you know about them?
Aren't you anxious?"

"I have come to know now,
I never told her, all this, to do,
I don't know anything much,
I am yet to know who is who."

"Your freedom, this is the first shock,
Do you think what she is saying is correct?
I don't know how many more shocks,
We may have to regret."

Thought the father, let us meet the boys parents,
It appears this girl will make us revolve,
If the boy is not good,
It may not become a problem, difficult to solve.

The son tried to fix a meeting,
The boys father was very casual and almost ill-treating,
He said, "Son's marriage!
At this age!"

The girl's brother finally requested,
The meeting was fixed,
The girl's father was reluctant to go,
But, he had to go.

The boy's parents were big businessmen,
Before them, they felt very small,
The house was big and beautifully decorated,
Before them, as if girl's parents were forced to fall.

The behaviour of the boy's parents was not good,
And the way before them they stood,
In a rude tone the father said, "Who wants to marry!
Our son, we don't want to marry!"

"He is not of age,
To marry, this is not the proper stage,
We will think when he is of a marriageable age,
Let him enjoy, I don't want to put him in cage."

*****

- ***SHOULD ANYONE DO GOOD OR BAD, WHICH EVERYONE IS DOING? IT REQUIRES COURAGE AND INTELLECT TO BE APART FROM OTHERS.***
- ***SHOULDN'T THE CHILDREN THINK OF PARENT'S PRESTIGE?***
- ***BLIND LOVE IS NO LOVE.***

*****

Said the boy's father, "We have to think about the family status,
We would like a family, who could face us,
And there are many in the race,
Many with bright face."

Said the girl's father, "The boy and the girl like each other,
They want to marry,
That is why we have come,
For us it is a matter to worry."

"Who wants to marry whom?
My son likes many,
Do you think he would marry everyone?
It looks funny."

"The boy has promised,
That is why we are here,
Kindly ask your son,
He might be somewhere near."

"There is no need to call the boy,
If you say, I will call,
He is too young to take decisions,
His age is to remain busy with cricket and tennis ball."

Finally, the boy came,
He was strong built having fair complexion,
He looked towards them and then turned his face,
He didn't wish to pay any attention.

"Papa, did you call me,
I was a little busy,"
"Yes, I did call you,
Please sit and take it easy."

The father told him the whole story,
As if for them it was a matter of great glory,
The boy with great attention, everything he did hear,
On his face there was no fear.

He said, "No doubt, we are friends,
But like her, I have many friends,
About marriage, I have not at all promised,
To think about this idea, I am not at all prepared."

"I think she is mistaken,
Like this, how can it happen?
We friends don't think like this,
We are friends, her or his."

On hearing this, the girl's father was badly shaken,
He started sweating,
He could not speak properly,
His lips and hands started trembling.

The boy immediately after saying left the place,
The boy's father was looking at their faces,
There was a sudden silence,
As if he was very happy after serving many aces.

The girl's brother said, "I think there is some misunderstanding,
We came to know that the boy was serious,"
He could not say anything further,
As he was also somewhat nervous.

"Make your girl understand properly,
She should forget the boy, may be slowly,
About marriage, the question doesn't arise,
For me, it was a great surprise."

*****

- ***BEFORE TAKING A DECISION REGARDING MARRIAGE, MAKE SURE, IS IT REAL LOVE OR LUST?***
- ***A SINCERE ADVICE GIVEN AND TAKEN SINCERELY CAN SOLVE MANY FUTURE PROBLEMS.***
- ***IF YOU SAY, NOTHING WILL HAPPEN, BE PREPARED FOR, IF SOMETHING MAY HAPPEN.***

*****

After saying this the boy's father got up,
Looking at him, they also got up,
The meeting was thus over,
And from the boy's side, the matter was closed forever.

But at the girl's side, the matter was not over,
They were down with some sort of fever,
They went back home disturbed,
The father went into deep silence, perturbed.

The brother told the whole story to the mother,
The girl was shocked,
Till now she thought, the boy was very sincere,
Tears started trickling down the eyes, the dreams were rocked.

The girl still wanted to talk to the boy,
How could he change so much,
Till yesterday, he was so nice,
He is not a bad boy as such.

Is he an expert in acting?
In love, so much of cheating,
Such a behaviour, I never thought,
Such people, some lesson, they should be taught.

Perhaps, he was afraid of his father,
But, if I am not, why should he be?
When I can face my father,
Why can't he?

Thought the girl, tomorrow, let me meet,
But, how should I treat,
But, I don't want to lose him,
I can't think of leaving him.

In her thought, the mother interrupted, "What are you thinking?
Perhaps, you are thinking of meeting,"
"After all, what wrong I did?
And then he is not a kid."

Said the mother, "I will not let him escape like this,
The mistake is his,
Why should he have such a relation?
Perhaps, he doesn't expect any reaction."

"They don't know me,
Both the son and father, I will set them right,
What they think of themselves,
I will show them a bit of my bite."

"Let me find their weakness,
How to reach them,
In the meantime, you ask him, why he did so?
But at the same time, tell him that he is a gem."

The girl meets the boy the next day,
The girl talks to the boy as usual,
Asks him about the yesterday's meeting,
And found his attitude very casceal.

"Didn't you promise me?
You said that for me you could die,
Then why did you insult my father and brother?
I just want to ask, why?"

"Even now, I say the same,
Marriage is not everything,
I love you,
In between, why your parents you bring."

*****

- ***ONE DAY, EVERYONE HAS TO PAY FOR HIS MISDEEDS.***
- ***ADD TO YOUR VIRTUES, NOT VICES, FOR A BETTER FUTURE.***
- ***MONEY CAN'T BUY POLITENESS AND VALUES.***

*****

As per mother's instructions, the girl did not prolong the discussion,
Started talking about other matters,
She didn't want to lose the boy,
Better to wait till the situation betters.

The girl couldn't control herself,
She knew, he was playing a love game,
She was now aware; the boy was not serious,
Him, she still wanted to tame.

Who gave her all the courage?
Perhaps, the mother and that within rage,
She knew, the boy has deceived,
She still hoped that the situation could be retrieved.

In the mind of her minds, she was weeping,
What she did, she was repenting,
She could not judge, her decision was hasty,
Within she was feeling guilty.

Perhaps, my father was right,
I never heard to his advice,
He is so soft, but wise,
After everything, with me he is so nice.

The mother engaged herself in finding about the family,
What is their business?
What were they doing earlier?
Their strengths and weaknesses, she started to assess.

Through the friends, she got into some connection,
Started getting some information,
They were not so rich earlier,
But, what was their business was not so clear.

Finally, she got in touch with their earlier neighbour,
In the name of her girl's marriage, she continued in her endeavour,
She came to know, some of their activities were not lawful,
She became hopeful.

She used her earlier government connections,
With them she still had friendly relations,
She reached a senior police officer,
To put pressure on boy's father.

In such matters she was an adept,
After knowing everything, this relation she was ready to accept,
In them, what was she looking for?
Insult, anger, money, she was at war.

It would take sometime,
I am not doing any crime,
I have to save my girl's life,
Otherwise, this affair would haunt her; hurt her with a knife.

The boy's father was advised,
He was pressurized,
It was difficult to make him agree,
But some problems, he did see.

He approached that officer back,
Money power, he did not lack,
But the official was also quite strong,
He told him bluntly that he and his son were wrong.

The officer warned him of dire consequences,
The boy's father applied his forces,
But, the officer could place him in a tight spot,
He started thinking, in a whirl; he may not be caught.

*****

- ***A WRONG STEP TAKEN ONCE MAY GET YOU IN TO A VICIOUS CIRCLE.***
- ***ALERTNESS PAYS IN LIFE.***
- ***BEFORE TRAPS, TRAP YOU; TRY TO FORESEE.***

*****

Perhaps, the boy's father then thought,
Right now, why get caught?
Why not accept the girl?
Otherwise, she is quite a pearl.

Later, we will deal,
Let this situation; a little heal,
The girl we will see how to treat,
I will then make them retreat.

I will make them see stars in the day,
That is the best way,
He, therefore, accepted,
The girl and the mother felt elated.

On hearing, the son and the father got confused,
The offer from the boy's side, they had never supposed,
The father tried to guess,
From the mother's face, something he did assess.

He asked the mother about it,
With happiness her face got lit,
"I have done,
This game I have won."

"Do you think marriage is a game?
Can you capture people like this in a frame?"
"If their son thinks, it is a play,
Then I want to show, I am not made of clay."

"Those people are not good,
We should not go in for such a relation,"
"My girl wants to marry him,
I don't want to see her in vexation."

"What about the later problems?
She will be in their house,"
"Later problems, I will see,
My girl is not a mouse."

"We can get another boy,
Later on, we may not have to weep,"
"There is nothing to think now,
The impact on girl's mind is quite deep."

"So, it's all final,
What do you say, dear son,"
"When the mother and girl are so sure,
Let us take it, that we have won."

In this situation, the father could not do much,
No one was that happy as such,
Who is responsible for this situation?
Would it bring peace or devastation?

The marriage was fixed,
Fear and happiness got mixed,
Minds on both the sides were disturbed,
The girl's father was somewhat perturbed.

At the marriage, the usual gay atmosphere was missing,
Instead of talks, people were hissing,
It looked more to be some job to be done,
All the rites were dutifully performed by the father and the son.

The marriage ceremony was over,
The girl was now with her in-laws,
The atmosphere was quite cool,
But, someone in the house was feeling that she is now in his claws.

*****

- ***WHEN THE KNIVES OF ANGER AND PRIDE ARE AT WORK, ANYONE CAN GET WOUNDED.***
- ***THE WEAKER THE FOUNDATIONS, THE WEAKER THE STRUCTURES.***
- ***AFTER WRONGDOINGS, THE RIGHT PATHS ARE ALWAYS AVAILABLE.***

*****

I met a friend of mine,
He didn't look so fine,
Asked him the reason,
Said, for him it was not a good season.

"I want my daughter to marry,
That is my main worry,
I have tried many places,
Seen many faces."

"She wants an ace,
Wants to remain number one in race,
In business, I want more money, more success,
Otherwise, in comforts, we have in excess, no less."

Increased desires will reduce happiness; will give you pain,
Discipline the desires, lost happiness, you will regain,
Want to continue with the desires, wait for the proper day,
Best, surrender before Him; the happiness will definitely stay.

FIVE

At the girl's in-laws, there was not much enthusiasm,
In one corner, the girl sat,
There was no welcome,
With her there was no one to chat.

The girl was now feeling lonely,
The husband was also not to be seen,
People were busy in their own talks,
To talk to someone, she was now keen.

In the house, the girl only thought of adjustment,
Still, she was not getting proper treatment,
With her husband, she was getting along nicely,
But her father and mother-in-law, whenever they talked, talked curtly.

The mother-in-law was proud of the wealth she possessed,
As per the property and wealth, everyone she assessed,
Her daughter-in-law, she didn't like,
She was always in a mood to strike.

By nature, she was haughty,
Took lot of care to maintain her beauty,
For money, she had great hunger,
People with less money, she would call, beggar.

For her, money was everything,
Money could buy anything,
This girl, she considered not rich, only middle class,
The less dowry she had brought was a great loss.

She was now preparing for an attack,
The husband-wife relationship, she was trying to crack,
With her husband, she was planning,
For the proper time, she was waiting.

The couple was enjoying, one night they came late,
This got added to her hate,
This was enough to start,
She considered scolding and embarrassing others, a useful art.

Next morning, the girl she hit,
"Now you are old enough, better take some responsibility,
Why were you late yesterday?
Like this don't become a liability."

"I told him to be in time,
But he didn't hear,
You can ask him,
Better, if things are clear."

"Listen, I don't want answers,
You have just to follow the instructions,
Don't tell me anything about my son,
And don't try to make corrections."

"I was just trying to explain,
I wanted to make everything clear,
Can't I talk?
I don't know, why you don't want to hear?"

"I think you, too much, like talking,
But I am not interested in hearing,
In this house, you better know your place,
And don't unnecessarily show me your face."

The son interrupted and took the girl to her room,
And told the girl to be cool,
"It's no use fighting with my mother,
She would always make you a fool."

*****

- ***CAN ONE GET LOVE BY FORCE?***
- ***MISDEEDS CAN BRING MOMENTARY HAPPINESS ONLY.***
- ***A HUMAN BEING IS ONLY A HUMAN BEING, WHETHER WITH MONEY OR WITHOUT MONEY.***

*****

"But I am not a fool,
Like this, no one can make me a tool,
Knowing my place, what does she want to tell?
I also know, how to yell."

"It was only you, who wanted to marry me,
Now, you have to adjust yourself,
In future also, be prepared for adjustments,
No one will, only you have to change yourself."

"Let us see who changes whom,
I will see to it,
No one knows me,
My mother has taught me how to hit."

"So your mother has taught you hitting,
Then, I don't think, you know anything about adjusting,
I think you are calling trouble for you,
Here, who can save you?"

"I only depend on you,
You have to save, who else I can say,
I am now your wife,
You have to be with me, there is no other way."

"Don't depend too much on me,
It was your choice,
Don't have too much trust in me,
And like this, don't raise your voice."

"So your wife, you will betray,
I love you, now, why don't you say,
It is only because of you, here, I can stay,
For me, there is no other way."

"What is there in saying?
I have so many girl friends, all-loving,
The only difference, you are at home,
They are outside home."

"So, you will carry on with your girl friends,
For you, now that road ends,
With your wife, you have to be sincere,
I would not allow anyone else to be near."

"How can I leave them?
They are still my friends,
They will remain my friends,
Such roads have no ends."

"I don't know, what are you talking,
You still don't understand, what is marriage?
Behave in a responsible manner,
You are not a kid, by age."

"You can't change me like this,
I will do what I want,
Any method, you may adopt,
Any device, you may plant."

"Like this, at least, you shouldn't behave,
You have started ill-treating, from others, how would you save?
Am I so bad?
Misbehaving with me here, everyone is so glad."

"I told you to remain cool,
That way is the best,
You have to control yourself,
And better adjust."

*****

- ***WHEN VICES CLUB TOGETHER, YOU MAY GET UNBEARABLE WOUNDS.***
- ***IF YOU FEEL YOU ARE GOING TO GET WOUNDED, FIND REMEDIES FIRST.***
- ***LEARN TO BEAR THE PAIN OF THE WOUNDS. THEN, NO ONE CAN DEFEAT YOU.***

*****

The girl with tears, went aside,
Everything she had to abide,
She felt, for everything she has to say yes,
She could have been at a better place, as otherwise the girl was no less.

One may call it circumstances,
One may call it fate,
But the actions done, on her mind's and sense's instructions,
She would herself hate.

There was no other remedy,
But to keep calm,
If she raised her voice,
There could be more harm.

The foundation of marriage is sincere love,
If the sincerity is missing,
Can it be called marriage?
It is like two strangers, in the same boat, just sailing.

Marriage is an association of the two,
The association is expected to remain till the end,
In between, let there be hurdles and problems,
Which both have to attend, let there be bends or a bend.

The attractions bring the two together,
The attractions and good thinking keep them together, whatever be the weather,
It is the senses and thoughts that bring them near,
And it is the senses and thoughts that make the relation tear.

Amid attractions and love,
What brings in hate in between?
An analysis of the causes of hate,
Can change the whole scene.

The analysis has to be unbiased,
The analysis has to be on both sides,
The analysis has to be sincerity based,
This can axe every hurdle that divides.

But there are divisions,
At that time, where are the attractions,
It is the mind that creates,
And it is the mind that deviates.

Apart from mind, there is a soul within every being,
What does the soul say?
The souls in the two beings are connected by an invisible string,
Naturally they say, better together stay.

It requires mind's mending,
It requires a little bending,
If the factors are nature born, it requires tolerance,
It requires not separation but endurance.

In her house, the girl was feeling alone,
There was on one, she could call her own,
She depended a lot on her husband,
Never expected, like this, her husband would disown.

You may call your wife a wife,
But, put in your attitude a knife,
Can it be called owning?
Doesn't that amount to disowning?

The husband should care for wife's feelings,
And the wife for husband's feelings,
When husband brings the wife to his house,
Shouldn't he be prepared to listen to her grouse?

*****

- ***FIGHT FOR YOUR RIGHTS, USING POSITIVE WAYS.***
- ***WHATEVER HAS HAPPENED HAS HAPPENED. ACCEPT IT, TO MAINTAIN PEACE.***
- ***ONE'S FUTURE PLANS SHOULD BE TO MAKE NOT TO BREAK.***

*****

The boy's parents were against the girl,
The boy, perhaps didn't know the meaning of marrying,
He said, he loved, but didn't care for her feelings,
In the name of love, he was betraying.

The girl went back home,
Told the facts to her mother,
Within she was weeping,
Had no guts to face the father.

The mother again thought of using her tactics,
She first thought, her son-in-law to handle,
Once he turns good,
Then the parents, she would tackle.

But the boy was very close to his parents,
By this time, the boy's father had made everything all right,
Used his money power,
And was now prepared for the fight.

The girl's mother again applied her ways,
Remembering, the success she got in earlier days,
But, this time the same officer did not care,
And said that it was their internal affair.

"Now the girl is married,
Sooner or later, the hate would be buried,
Interfering can be damaging,
The problems, the girl would be managing."

The mother had now no other way left,
Peace and happiness, there was a great theft,
Using wrong ways, one wants success,
And then waits, for goodness.

When one takes a wrong path,
May feel happy, for sometime, with the results,
But with changing situations,
From the nature, he may get stronger assaults.

It depends on one's mind's working,
The decision, on right and wrong thinking,
Certain past impressions, may take someone to wickedness,
The same mind, under the influence of proper guidance can turn to goodness.

The guidance can be from scriptures,
The past impressions can change as a whole,
The guidance can be from a learned person,
But the best is one which one gets from its own soul.

The girl is the sufferer,
She is suffering because of her own deeds,
The mother also got swayed,
But, the effect is on the life one leads.

The girl went back to her in-laws,
She was almost in a depressed state,
No help was coming from any direction,
Even small matters would irritate.

At the in-laws, the father, mother and the son,
The girl, they would just ignore,
She should never feel at home,
The girl sensed, for her, there was a big trouble in store.

She tried to change her husband,
But he was with his parents,
At times, the behaviour was quite cruel,
She was ill-treated like servants.

*****

- ***AFTER CERTAIN MISTAKES, ALL THE PATHS AROUND BECOME DIM AND DARK.***
- ***IMPURE MINDS, IMPURE DECISIONS.***
- ***A STABLE AND PURE MIND IS BETTER EQUIPPED TO FACE THE TROUBLES.***

*****

The mother-in-law had the dowry factor also in mind,
Which she used to again and again remind,
Over dowry, she would become very rude,
Her language was becoming more and more crude.

The girl tried to fight,
But to fight, she had no right,
Had she come to her in-laws on their choice,
She could have better raised her voice.

But, the struggle, she continued,
Not to win, but just to exist,
The attacks of her mother-in-law,
She could not resist.

Now, she remembered her pre-marriage days at home,
Her ways, the father opposed,
She thought him to be wrong,
Old thinking, she supposed.

In the early youth, some children make such blunders,
The mind just wanders,
Think that, only they are correct,
Others advice, just reject.

As she got up in the morning,
A fear occupied her feeling,
A fear of embarrassment,
A feeling of resentment.

She liked her husband,
But, he was not sincere as yet,
That was her main problem,
At times, made her eyes wet:

The mother, father and brother could not do anything,
They dare not interfere,
There was an atmosphere of gloom in their house,
They were living in some sort of fear.

A fear that she may not be harmed,
A fear of some sort of an assault,
They used to think of her tenderness,
And the way she was facing insult.

The mother who thought herself to be too great,
Was also in sobs,
She was too proud and confident,
This is how, the pride, the time robs.

The mother-in-law had by now become too cruel,
Together with son and husband, she knew how to rule,
The girl did all the domestic work,
She had just been made a tool.

It was the month of August,
The festival of Raksha Bandhan was coming near,
On that day, the girl wanted to go home,
The mother-in-law may not play a game; there was some fear.

She told her mother-in-law in advance,
She didn't want to take any chance,
On telling her, she remained mum,
On repeating, she just said, "Hum."

On the day before the occasion,
She told her a number of tasks for the next day,
Told her that guests were coming,
And till the guests were there, the daughter-in-law had to stay.

*****

- ***WHEN THINGS GO AWRY, GOD'S CONTEMPLATION PROVIDES INSPIRATION AND CONFIDENCE.***
- ***EXCESSIVE WEALTH BREEDS EXCESSIVE PRIDE, WHY?***
- ***CRUELTY IS THE OFF SPRING OF ANGER AND LUST.***

*****

The girl took it positively,
Thought that she would go a little late,
But the guests didn't arrive till afternoon,
Now, it looked that some problem she is going to create.

As the day passed off,
The girl became very anxious,
At last, the guests arrived late in the afternoon,
The girl was sad and serious.

It seemed the mother-in-law was looking for such a chance,
The girl's sad face, she was enjoying,
With her guests, she got busy,
She was just laughing and talking.

For the girl, no one cared,
At her, they awkwardly stared,
She continued to serve,
Having control at her nerve.

And then came her brother's phone,
The mother-in-law spoke to him in different tone,
And told him that she was busy,
"She would come, take it easy."

The daughter-in-law wanted to go in the morning,
It was now evening,
The mother-in-law had something different in mind,
The money power and the earlier events had made her blind.

The girl was bringing something hot in her hands,
She was coming towards the main hall,
The mother-in-law deliberately gave her a hard push,
The hot stuff splashed on her, she had a bad fall.

All got up,
The girl was almost crying,
But, no one gave her a helping hand,
"Get up, I suppose, you are not dying."

The girl tried to get up,
But could not,
She now started weeping bitterly,
The stuff she was carrying was quite hot.

Hearing the noises,
Came her husband,
"What has happened?"
And gave her a helping hand.

The other ladies just watched,
One or two even laughed,
The mother-in-law just remained silent,
Thinking happily, that today she has made a dent.

The girl still could not get up,
Perhaps, she had broken one of her bones,
Now came up the ladies,
And started talking in different tones.

Do dresses, jewelry and money, makes someone so high?
That even social values, he or she can buy,
Money, no doubt, plays an important function,
But, does that distort man-to-man relation?

Money, at times, makes a man rude,
It changes one's attitude,
It rarely softens,
It mostly hardens.

*****

- ***WHEN A BAD DEED IS COOKED UP IN THE MIND, THE SOUL, THE GOD'S PART, JUST WATCHES AND PASSES IT ON TO THE ALMIGHTY.***
- ***BEFORE A MISDEED, THINK TWICE, GOD IS WITHIN YOU IN THE SHAPE OF THE SOUL. NATURE'S LAW MAY NOT PROSECUTE YOU.***
- ***OTHERS FALL AMUSES A CRUEL MIND.***

*****

Money, so important for living,
Is a God's gift,
The hunger for which,
May become the source of a severe rift.

Money only God can provide,
Getting, a mind, as if, goes on a happy ride,
Getting this God's gift, why harden?
Why not soften?

Why not give money to the needy?
Why become more and more greedy?
If the man considers God as good,
The money should do no harm, but only good.

At times, it makes a person ill-treat,
At mind it makes a person less neat,
Is the money responsible for that extra pride within?
It sprouts that pride within!

If a man becomes rich,
And at the same time, he is awakened within,
He becomes wise within,
Then, the desire to help others, comes somewhere from within.

But when an unwise becomes rich,
Whose mind is shrouded in darkness of ignorance,
He feels, he has become very strong and big,
In fact, he lacks consciousness and proper sense.

The girl was surrounded by all such people,
She was in pain and trouble,
The husband picked her up and took her to the bedroom,
With sorrow and shock, she had become pale.

She had to be taken to the hospital,
She had broken a bone and had to be plastered,
It was then night,
The girl's parents were informed.

The parents came running,
Confused and burning,
Thinking, the girl is being tortured,
Mother's eyes with tears, blurred.

Said the father in sad tone, "You didn't listen to me,
Now, she is placed in a bad situation,
Warned you,
Now, you see her condition."

The mother remained silent,
She was in a pensive mood,
Thinking, they are so bad,
Such idea, I never had.

The parents reached the hospital,
Alone, the girl was lying,
Even the husband was not there,
Seeing the mother, started sobbing and crying.

Asked the mother, " What happened?"
"I was pushed,"
"Who pushed?"
"My mother-in-law deliberately pushed."

"I was carrying something hot,
She came from somewhere,
And just pushed,
I fell down, how I am not aware."

*****

- *MONEY WITH PRUDENCE AND SATISFACTION IS A REAL NATURE'S GIFT.*
- *TAKE CARE, MONEY IS DANGEROUS TOO.*
- *MONEY IS A GREAT PEACE THIEF.*

*****

"Here my husband brought me,"
"But, where is he?"
"He has gone to bring some medicines,"
"He will have to pay for his sins."

"I will see to them,
The police, we can inform,"
"Please don't do that,
That may do more harm."

The girl who was so bold before marriage,
Had lost her courage and confidence,
The mother thought her to be strong,
But, she could not put any resistance.

The entire family was disturbed,
The relation, they didn't want to break,
The girl was being harassed,
They were thinking, what action they should take.

In the meantime, came the boy,
His mood didn't look to be bad,
Because of the day's incident,
He didn't look sad.

Asked the father, "What happened?"
"She had a very bad fall,
I don't know,
She fell while she was coming to the hall."

No one asked, who pushed whom,
They knew, it would bring doom,
The mother was boiling with anger, but remained silent,
She didn't want to enter into any argument.

It was 9.30 pm, the rakhi, on her brother, she tied,
A little, the girl smiled, seemed a young flower dried,
Again started weeping,
Some fear within was creeping.

It was 10.30 pm, came the boy's parents,
No worry, both laughing and talking,
As they came near, changed their expressions,
Artificial faces, hardly smiling.

Asked the mother-in-law, "How are you now?
Get up now,
What happened?
I hope the doctors have attended."

Told the son, "Her leg has been plastered,
For a month she has been advised bed rest,
It may take even more than a month,
Proper diet and care, the doctor did suggest."

"She has done the mistake,
How are we responsible?
Let her remain at mother's place,
Come back, to do some work, when capable."

The girl's mother could not resist,
Those words, she could not digest,
She said forcefully, "How is she responsible?
To do any work, she is capable."

"Don't you listen; she has done a mistake,
Actually, she is not used to polished surfaces,
She had a bad fall,
She thought she has to take part in races."

*****

- ***WRONG STEPS TAKEN IN THE YOUTH, HAUNT TILL THE END OF ONE'S LIFE.***
- ***NOT GOD, MAN'S MIND IS DANGEROUS.***
- ***TRY TO LOOK THROUGH THE MASKS.***

*****

"She is used to surfaces and races,
But not used to a family like yours,
In-laws can be so bad,
She is just in tears."

"The girl is not good for anything,
To marry, we were not interested,
Only you forced,
Even my son never wanted."

"It was your son, into a trap, who lured,
It was he, the game he played,
Now don't try to be innocent,
Like this, people just try to become decent."

"I know how much decent you are,
You can't even maintain a good car,
It is the wealth that plays the real role,
It is our wealth, she wants to control."

"How do you know she is after money?
She has seen enough of it at her place,
I don't know why she went for this boy,
People having no grace."

"Enough of it at her place,
With her, what has she brought?
All useless things,
They are all getting rot."

"So you are after dowry also,
And that is the main cause of irritation,
That is the real problem,
And that is why she is in this situation."

"She is in this situation, because of her own actions,
With us, she was not fit to have relations,
You should have thought of it before,
I don't want to tolerate her any more."

"This situation is because of your pushing,
To put her in trouble was your planning,
Instead of a case of burning,
It is a case of pushing."

"It is no use blaming me,
I just want to make her free,
You may keep on speaking,
And anyone may keep on hearing."

"You will have to hear,
And you have to bear,
A few days ago your son got married,
And now you say, the marriage stands buried."

"My son will do, what I say,
He is not yet that mature,
The whole day, he is not at home,
For her, we don't have any cure."

"He can't wash his hands of like this,
The responsibility is his,
Specially, when you have pushed,
And her fall, you have planned."

"I don't know, what you are talking,
How can I make her fall?
She is not so small,
Neither she is a doll."

*****

- ***ATROCITIES COMMITTED AGAINST THE WEAK AND THE POOR MAY NOT BE TREATED AS BRAVERY.***
- ***BRAVERY LIES IN ACCEPTING PEOPLE AND TO COEXIST.***
- ***A HUMAN BEING SHOULD BE TREATED AS A HUMAN BEING, WHETHER YOUR DAUGHTER OR DAUGHTER-IN- LAW.***

*****

"So you want some proof,
Because you know, the only witness is your roof,
But why should, she tell a lie,
In your hands, one day she may not die."

"That is why, her, I don't want to keep,
She will unnecessarily weep,
Against me, she will again complain,
And I am not in a habit to explain."

"Is she your daughter-in-law or your servant?
You just hire and then fire,
Your son has spoiled her life,
He is a big liar."

"You are just after my son,
What have we done?
We don't like her,
And we don't want to keep her."

"Then let her, to the police, make a statement,
You will be in trouble,
I am not going to leave you like this,
You can't crush us like a bubble."

"This also you may try,
Before the police also, let her lie,
I am a hard nut to crack,
And I know, how to make others cry."

"Your son is responsible,
He has to provide her care and shelter,
The girl, your son has married,
Just marry to leave her later."

"He has married,
Up till here, her, he has carried,
Now if he doesn't want to keep any relation,
What can you do in that situation?"

"So you have left all gentleness,
Height of shamelessness,
With people like you, what will happen to our society?
Don't you have any fear of the deity?"

"How does the God come in between?
And I am not afraid of anyone,
I go to temple everyday,
And what have I done?"

"Your daughter-in-law, you are harassing,
You are making her life difficult,
Every moment you are putting her in trouble,
This you are doing, as per which religion or cult."

"I don't know about all these things,
But, I know your own daughter-in-law; you are ill-treating,
Then, why these questions?
That way, I should also start you questioning."

"That is my internal affair,
Don't give it so much air,
Right now, I am talking about my daughter,
The topic, don't alter."

"So you treat your daughter and daughter-in-law differently,
About your daughter, you are so much worried,
Better, keep her with you,
To live with us, she is now somewhat scared."

*****

- ***CAN ONE WASH OFF THE SINS BY JUST GOING TO A TEMPLE?***
- ***BURY THE HATE, BEFORE IT IS TOO LATE.***
- ***REVENGE MAY NOT MAKE YOU A CRIMINAL AS PER THE HUMAN'S LAW OR AS PER THE NATURE'S LAW.***

*****

"How to scare young people like this, you very well know,
But, why this girl?
Has the girl ever insulted you?
Then why at her, insults you are ready to hurl?"

"On this issue, I don't want to speak anymore,
For her, I have shut my door,
The best solution is divorce,
Now you can't get help from any source."

"You have enmity with me,
Towards her, why don't you leave the hostility?
You ask your son,
They love each other, he knows the reality."

"Us, you wanted to destroy,
It was all because of my innocent boy,
Now, why are you begging?
After sometime you will also start weeping."

"See, past is past,
Now, we can be good friends,
Let us forget the past,
This hostility can have an end, upon you it depends."

"So, you are now changing colors,
You are talking about friendliness,
I can understand very well,
I can see the seriousness."

"Let us think peacefully,
Let them stay together,
Let us sit and talk,
Our relations can be better."

"You want to forget the past,
But I can't forget,
By forgetting the past,
Peace, will I get?"

"It depends upon you,
What more can I say,
Whatever has happened, has happened,
Let us treat it as nature's play."

"It was not nature's,
It was your play,
And what, you are talking,
It's only a ploy."

"See, you don't have a daughter,
It is difficult to see a daughter in pain,
You feel from my angle,
Arguments and arguments will not be of any gain."

"Your daughter-in-law is also someone's daughter,
With her, how are you behaving?
Why so much difference?
I know the relations, you are having."

"That is a different story,
The circumstances are different,
Why bring in that?
The causes are different."

While she was talking,
The boy's father and mother alongwith the boy left in a hurry,
To anyone they didn't talk, while going,
The enmity, they didn't want to bury.

*****

- ***THE ANGER MAY LEAVE AN IRREPARABLE DENT.***
- ***TRY TO SEE IN YOUR MIND'S EYE, THE EFFECT OF ANGER ON OTHERS.***
- ***SOFTEN YOUR ATTITUDE BEFORE IT IS TOO LATE.***

*****

It was a dark evening,
I was going by the roadside,
Saw a tree had fallen,
The day's storm had taken it in its tide.

A big chunk of earth had come out,
The earth lay wounded,
There was no one to mourn the tree's death,
The earth's wound, no one was astounded.

The earth gets wounded, day and night,
No one feels or cares,
No one knows the pain,
The sky also just stares.

The earth loves and cares everyone,
Its fruits, everyone eats,
We crush it every moment,
And in any way anyone treats.

Thought I, of earth I am born,
Must learn from her that fairness,
That patience and generosity,
And, above all, the quality of forgiveness.

SIX

That incident left the father, mother and the brother vexed,
The mother felt like crying,
The brother and father serious,
The girl was sighing.

For the daughter, she left that pride,
On which she used to ride,
Still her in-laws didn't hear,
The pain was difficult to bear.

It is better never to fly so high,
It may make you one day weep and sigh,
The haughty mind makes so high a fly,
He forgets, the next moment he may die.

When a friend dies,
The mind suddenly saddens,
One starts thinking the meaning of life,
After sometime, forgets, again and again it happens.

Forgetting the sorrowful past is necessary,
But why forget the life's reality,
I am here for only sometime,
Why not remember this while bowing before the deity.

We are here only for sometime,
We have come here on lease,
The rent we have to pay,
Till the time we cease.

The rent payment is love and respect to others,
It is to take care of nature's objects,
It is not to deceive and trouble others,
All this, the untidy mind rejects.

The rent is to make others blossom,
To help others rise,
To make others more comfortable,
Not to make others feel that, I am bigger in size.

It is to respect others sincere feelings,
It is not to hurt others feelings,
It is to refrain from sins,
Also, to enjoy others wins.

Make yourself know the God's nature,
Know that every human being is a part of nature,
Understand that anyone's fall is fall of a part of nature,
And to make him rise is helping the nature.

You, me, he and others is all nature,
The God exists in every creature,
To abuse anyone is to abuse the nature,
Forget not, the witness is the soul within every creature.

The payment of rent is necessary,
Rather, non-payment, going against the nature, is an offence,
The punishment may be as per the crime,
Every crime, our mind is well equipped to sense.

Nature is all-powerful,
Make efforts to be lawful,
Ignorance is no excuse,
You may not reach a stage; any help God may refuse.

First, educate your own self,
Educate your young ones,
To educate and shape the young at an early stage is one's duty,
If possible, educate the ignorant ones.

*****

- ***GIVE HAPPINESS AND YOU WILL GET HAPPINESS.***
- ***YOU CAN'T HIDE FROM, DECEIVE, OR DODGE THE NATURE.***
- ***YOU MAY NOT HAVE TO PAY YOUR RENT ARREARS IN YOUR NEXT BIRTH.***

*****

The penalties can be soft and hard,
It can at times be destruction,
Can be problems and troubles,
It can also be an obstruction.

Only He can excuse the penalties,
Only He can reduce the penalties,
Therefore, be close to Him,
Meditate on Him.

He would give you the strength to remain away from the sins,
Your mind, He would purify,
The lust, anger and pride would get greatly subdued,
Then, the nature's laws, you would not defy.

He would tell you the path to walk,
He would give you the words to talk,
He would give you the needed success,
If not success, then the way to remain in peace in distress.

He is the world's best guide,
By His nature's laws just abide,
The pain and sorrows would slowly die,
When, to surrender completely before Him, you would decide.

Life is to let others live,
Better forgive,
Not to ill-treat,
Everyone, with soft words, one must greet.

Life is to accept, whatever has happened,
For the future, think of the betterment,
Strive, with peace, to improve,
But, for the present, think of adjustment.

Life is to make the relations,
Not to break the relations,
If possible, mend the relations,
Better, find some solutions.

Life is to understand each other,
To live in harmony,
Better invest love,
Think; peace can't be bought with money.

Life is not just to waste,
Want to take its full taste,
Without cause, don't take decisions in haste,
Rash and illogical decisions may not bring distaste.

Life is to remain peaceful,
To remain dutiful,
Not to be revengeful,
Be prepared to be regretful.

The girl, the girl's parents took her care,
About her future, they were not aware,
She was in her old room,
The family was in gloom.

From her in-laws, no one enquired,
About them no one talked,
On the bed, she was just lying,
In a pensive mood, no sobbing or crying.

The mother took all pains to make her stand,
With her, she was deeply attached,
The mother had no words to talk,
She just watched and watched.

*****

- ***A MAN IS COMPLETE, WHEN HE FULLY UNDERSTANDS HIM AND HIS NATURE.***
- ***SEARCH THE MEANING OF LIFE IN YOUR LIFE.***
- ***LET MIND NOT RULE YOU.***

*****

The girl was recovering from that severe attack,
Her leg was also recovering quite rapidly,
She wore a long silence,
After a few days started talking rather sadly.

All the wounds, with time, heal,
Bad days also, the times steal,
Physical wounds leave scars, visible,
Mind's wounds also leave scars, invisible.

When deeply attached to God,
The mind's wounds heal up easily,
Where the mind can talk to the soul,
The mind and body recover very rapidly.

It was winter,
The sun came and went,
The girl just stared out,
No message ever, her husband sent.

She just thought and thought,
In love, she had been deceived,
The mind was now repenting,
Sincere love, she never received.

The father, at times, used to console,
"You will go back to your in-laws again,
Things will change,
Don't just cry, in vain."

She knew, things were difficult to change,
But man lives on expectation,
Things may change,
Time may end this separation.

About the matter, she didn't want to talk to anyone,
Wanted to remain alone,
Even when the mother talked,
She remained mum like a stone.

For the mother, the pain was crossing the limits,
No remedy was visible,
She tried, but in vain,
No help was available.

She cursed the God,
She cursed the fate,
She talked about remarriage,
Looking at her young age and the hate.

She was in a difficult state,
On the one end, she was talking of remarrying,
The girl, she wanted to speak,
But, she simply refused talking.

Days were passing; things were not improving,
All this caused her great vexation,
The mother couldn't bear this downfall,
And was getting into depression.

With her daughter-in-law, she was not on speaking terms,
The daughter-in-law was, however, sympathetic,
She wanted to help,
Her approach was pragmatic.

About the mother's health, father was also worried,
But, his mind he could manage,
He had great faith in God,
Complete surrender to God, he had reached that stage.

*****

- ***POCKET HATE, PEACE IT WOULD TAKE.***
- ***IMPROPER MIND MANAGEMENT, DON'T CURSE THE FATE.***
- ***WALK ON THE PATH OF RIGHTEOUSNESS WITHOUT FEAR.***

*****

The mother had sleepless nights,
For all the happenings, she was holding herself responsible,
Within, she was haunted by the feelings of guilt,
Now, to do anything, she was not able.

The things were going from bad to worse,
One day she fell down while working,
She was rushed to the hospital,
From heart attack, she was suffering.

The younger son was watching all this,
He had completed his studies,
Was not getting job,
Wanted to go abroad for further studies.

The father told him to wait,
With the circumstances at home, he had developed some hate,
From these happenings, he wanted to run away,
To get away, he was finding a way.

The boy was deeply attached to the mother,
He used to remain very less with his father,
Study, study and study, that only he would hear,
With the worldly matters, he was not at all clear.

His studies were over,
Yet, he was not properly educated,
His mind was not mature,
In a confused state, he was situated.

A youngster should know, how to tackle a difficult situation?
He should know, how to control an emotion?
How to find a solution?
And how to take a proper decision?

He should be fully conversant with the values of life,
Should understand, what is patience?
Should know, how to be humble?
Should know the meaning and impact of arrogance.

Well-versed, where and how to act?
And where to react?
Where and what sort of language, he should use?
And the power, he should not abuse.

Should know, how to keep the anger within his teeth?
How not to make others angry?
How to be respectful?
And that for love and respect, everyone is hungry.

Should know, how to adjust within his means?
The meaning of contentment and satisfaction,
To wait peacefully till the flowers bloom,
For himself and others, not to be troublesome in action.

The father knew that the son needed proper guidance,
The mother did give love, but to face life, didn't train,
Till now, he was in his studies and studies,
It was now, that the problems had started to rain.

With the son, he argued and gave him suggestions,
At this stage, to him, the son listened,
The father acquainted him with different facets of life,
With all this, he seemed to have gained.

He was told to join hands with his brother,
Which, he gladly accepted,
He started learning the work,
Sister-in-law and the brother, both he respected.

*****

- ***EDUCATION IS NOT COMPLETE TILL THE MIND ATTAINS MATURITY.***
- ***THE FATHER AND THE MOTHER BOTH HAVE TO HELP AND GUIDE THE CHILD ATTAIN MATURITY.***
- ***THE PARENTS ARE FIRST EXPECTED TO KNOW THE VALUES AND THE MEANING OF MATURITY IN THE TRUE SENSE.***

*****

The mother not being well,
She would neither work nor speak,
With all these happenings, the father took the house's control,
These happenings could not make him weak.

He talked with the elder son and daughter-in-law,
What should be done, about the daughter?
How to save her future?
How to tackle the matter?

It was decided to speak to the boy privately,
And that the elder son and daughter-in-law meet the boy,
To discuss with him every aspect,
And to tell him that girl is not a toy.

Accordingly, both tried to meet the boy,
Since, it was decided to meet the boy privately,
They didn't ring up at home,
Outside the house, they tried to trace him secretly.

It was a difficult job to do,
But they were bent on finding a solution,
From the girl, they came to know, where he used to go,
And finally to meet, they located a situation.

The restaurant, he used to visit regularly,
Here, he was caught napping,
They grabbed the seat in front of him,
There was no chance of escaping.

They met him with smiles,
And at first told him that they were not his enemies,
"We just want to have friendly talk with you,
Right now, you may not even treat us as your relatives."

Uttered the daughter-in-law,
"Is everything alright?
Hope everything is fine,
We are not here to fight."

"Everything is fine,
But, right now, I have no time,
Someone, I have to meet,
For a treat."

"Won't you ask about your wife?
She remembers you day and night,
Don't you remember her?
Have you ever thought of her plight?"

"It's not like that,
I am sorry for the problems she had,
I have not forgotten,
It was all sad."

"What about her future?
Is it right to leave the girl like this in pain?
She even now hopes that you would come back,
It looks you have just left her slain."

"I have nothing to do with it,
It is my parents; they have some reasons,
I have to obey my parents,
They have some serious objections."

"Don't you think, you are doing something wrong?
Aren't you committing a sin?
What is her mistake?
Only because you are a boy, you want to win."

*****

- ***STRIVE TO MAKE YOUR CHILD A STRONG HUMAN BEING, NOT A BEAST.***
- ***NATURE MAY NOT ASK YOU, "WHY YOU MADE HIM A BEAST?"***
- ***DISTRIBUTE LOVE AND NOT MISERIES.***

*****

"I totally depend on my parents,
They know what to do and what not to do,
I have to follow them,
I do what they tell me to do."

"The girl is suffering because of you,
You have made her life a hell,
You can't wash of your hands like this,
To do all this, did your parents tell?"

"I am in a great hurry,
For me, someone is waiting,
I have given time to her,
Talk to my parents, with me, time you are wasting."

"Had someone properly guided you in your childhood,
Like this you would not have spoken,
You are a married boy not a kid,
This serious matter, so lightly you would not have taken."

"I have completed my education,
Now, with my father, I have to do business,
I am not a kid,
And for that, I am very serious."

"A girl you like,
You, enjoy and marry,
After some days, say goodbye,
And then do business and make merry."

"But, I married, took her home,
Now, with my mother, she didn't develop good relations,
What have I done?
For me, all these accusations."

"But, did you try to improve the relations?
Did you try to find solutions?
Did you give your parents some suggestions?
Then, why get worried about accusations?"

"No, I never did all that,
My mother is very angry,
And when she is in anger,
I don't speak, even if I am hungry."

"Only because of her anger, you are not speaking,
To the girl, you are doing such a great harm,
This mistake of yours,
You have created for her such a big storm."

The daughter-in-law was speaking very politely,
But at the same time very firmly,
In her approach, she was bold,
And knew, how and whatever was to be told.

At this the boy said, "If you hold me responsible,
What to do now?
Past is past, I can't do anything,
If I can help, how?"

"Your parents, you should convince,
It is just properly explaining,
You will tell them the truth only, nothing else,
It is, without fear expressing."

She further said, "You should have guts to narrate the truth,
A human being you are deceiving and hurting,
It is not only that a girl is crying and sobbing,
The soul within is also watching."

*****

- ***POLITENESS PAYS, PERSUASIVENESS STRENGTHENS.***
- ***POSITIVE BOLDNESS IS AN ASSET, WHICH COMES FROM WITHIN.***
- ***EMPATHY AND POLITENESS ARE THE TOOLS OF THE WISE AND THE BRAVE.***

*****

The daughter-in-law said, "Now stop meeting the other girls,
And do some good deeds,
Save this girl,
And this is what the hour needs."

"Life is a balance sheet of good and bad deeds,
The more you do good deeds,
The happier you will be,
If not today, tomorrow, the sorrow will follow the bad deeds."

"It is because of some good previous deeds,
That today, you are enjoying,
As soon as its account will finish,
You may not find yourself in difficulty and crying."

"I am sorry, I am telling you all this,
Your parents might have told you earlier,
But, had they, you should not have left the girl like this,
If in your mind, these facts were clear."

Said the brother, "I hope you have not misunderstood us,
We are your well-wishers,
I am sure both of you can live a happy life,
We can all become good friends."

"I thank you for showing the right path,
And for the awakening,
I will talk to my parents today itself,
And, then you, I will be informing."

THE SEVEN P'S OF AN EFFECTIVE PERSONALITY

- ***PROACTIVE***
- ***PLANNING***
- ***POLITE***
- ***PATIENT***
- ***PHYSICAL AND MIND POWER***
- ***PERSUASIVE***
- ***POSITIRE***

Seven

The entire discussion was told to the father,
The father was happy at whatever had been achieved,
And the role played by the daughter-in-law,
For which, from the father-in-law, great praise, she received.

But, in the evening, from the boy, came the telephone,
The boy was very dejected,
He could not achieve anything good,
All his arguments, parents rejected.

They were unhappy the way girl's mother tackled the situation,
And that they suffered great humiliation,
That, how could they forget?
The girl, they were not prepared to accept.

Said the boy, "I would continue my efforts,
I want to meet my wife, if you allow,
I don't want to commit more mistakes,
I don't want to give her any more trouble now."

Said the brother, "You come any time you want,
Here you will always be welcomed,
That would provide us great relief,
This is what we all desired."

The boy came the same day to meet his wife,
She could now walk and was alright,
She went out with her husband,
And that gave them great delight.

It was raining,
As if two hearts were singing,
But at the in-law's house, he didn't stay,
He wanted parents approval and told them to wait for that day.

The girl was somewhat happy,
The mother, on the bed, she was lying,
The daughter-in-law, whom she had rejected,
Was now helping and serving.

The mother-in-law was still in deep thoughts,
She was feeling very much embarrassed,
The daughter-in-law was happy serving,
But, was unaware, by her mother-in-law, when would she be embraced.

The daughter-in-law, was regularly attending the office,
She was also looking after the house responsibly,
The girl's attitude towards the daughter-in-law was changing,
With her she was becoming more and more friendly.

The mother-in-law's attitude was also changing,
Only at times of need, with the daughter-in-law, she was speaking,
Day and night, around her she was working,
Only, sometimes with her, she was smiling.

The overall atmosphere of the house was not good,
The girl, at times, felt very sad,
The boy would visit only sometimes,
He was having problems with his dad.

With his father, he had quarreled,
The atmosphere in that house was also tense,
They never wanted the girl back,
The father would say, "To bring her back there is no sense."

The boy had now changed his thinking,
He felt that his wife was his responsibility,
The mother and father were not agreeing,
To earn alone for his wife, he had no ability.

*****

- ***INVESTMENT OF LOVE BY THE DAUGHTER-IN-LAW CAN ENRICH THE HOUSE'S ENVIRONMENT.***
- ***THE MEMBERS OF THE HOUSE SHOULD ARRANGE AN ATMOSPHERE WHEREIN SHE CAN INVEST LOVE.***
- ***BEWARE; HATRED CAN BE VERY DANGEROUS. IT MAY MAKE YOU SICK.***

*****

He was a spoilt child,
When it was time to learn, he didn't learn,
He was busy with other jobs,
Now of his own, he wanted to earn.

Now, that he had come to senses,
He was perhaps, searching the meaning of life,
He had started feeling his responsibility,
And was thinking, always of supporting his wife.

He was always thinking and thinking,
When I was going the wrong path, why my parents didn't stop?
Why they didn't guide me properly?
Why in education, they didn't show me the path to reach the top?

The parents in their deep attachment towards the child,
Sometimes forget what is wrong and what is right,
The child might be beating and abusing someone,
But, at that time, that may give them delight.

As the child grows,
With his childhood habits, he may go astray,
In their attachment, the parents may not even know,
Till, with them he starts misbehaving and starts to disobey.

Their arrogance, some of them, may neglect,
Child's arrogance, some of them may accept,
One day the parents will have to weep,
When the worms of wrong thinking have seated themselves in the child very deep.

The problem arises, when the child becomes an adult,
Their deep attachment, leading to neglect, starts showing its color,
When the child becomes rude, curt and a wrongdoer,
Till then they take his actions as valour.

Even then, they may not think it's their mistake,
Some other reason they may give, or fate they may call,
At that time, counseling may or may not help,
And the problem may become very tall.

Lack of care at the parents end,
May one day take the form of a thought or deed that is evil,
Later, they may repent,
When they see their child as a devil.

To become a parent, it is easy,
In that daily struggle for life, one gets busy,
But the responsibilities of the parenthood,
Will have to be clearly understood.

On the thinking of the child, the parents will have to keep a close watch,
First the parents will have to learn and decide about the good and bad deeds,
And then on his actions, a careful watch,
Will have to correct his actions, whenever the situation needs.

Sometimes, the parents can't envisage,
What the child's thinking and actions will lead to?
With the present thinking, what kind of man, he could become?
When he becomes an adult, what would he do?

The clarity in the parents mind is necessary,
And both, the father and mother must agree,
Many cases, there is disagreement,
One thing, they would agree, their child, a good personality they want to see.

The parents want their child to obey them,
From the child, they expect respect,
Shape his personality, when very young,
Should not forget this aspect.

*****

- ***YOU CAN SHAPE YOUR CHILD'S PERSONALITY.***
- ***ENVISION YOUR CHILD'S BEHAVIOR, TEN YEARS HENCE.***
- ***CHANGE YOUR CHILD WITH LOVE AND REASONING, NOT BY FORCE. CONVINCE HIM WITH PROPER LOGIC.***

*****

If they want respect,
When he is an adult,
They should themselves be good beings,
Otherwise, they may not get the desired result.

They have themselves, first, to keep away from wrongdoing,
The wrongdoing, the child, it may attract,
They have no right to find faults in their child,
If they have forgotten this life's facet.

To make the child a good human being,
Is not easily achievable,
Many problems and difficulties will stop the path,
But, with parent's right thinking, is possible.

You may train, a bad company, he may get into,
A constant watch, his mind may not go ill,
Your training can mend others also,
All this, you need a strong will.

First to make ourselves good and then our child,
If, to this, all of us agree,
The vice may almost vanish,
All virtues on this earth, we may see.

The boy with his wife, now he wanted to settle,
Within, he was fighting a battle,
With the parents, he argurd; he couldn't succeed,
With his views, they never agreed.

The boy had now become restless,
He was unhappy, with the parent's role,
One night, when the parents were sleeping,
A good amount of cash, he stole.

The next morning, he went out early,
And didn't come back, in the evening,
The parents waited and waited, but he didn't return,
They were surprised to see their cash missing, next
morning.

They rang up the girl's house,
Spoke in an angry tone,
The voice from the other side was not soft,
It said, " Nothing is known."

The boy's parents got worried,
The police was informed,
For many days, the boy remained missing,
The police and parents kept guessing.

One fine morning, the girl received a telegram,
Informed, with a friend, he was staying,
To do some course, he was thinking,
Will come back, when he starts earning.

The girl was somewhat sad, and somewhat happy,
She was helpless, couldn't do anything,
But she also thought of studying,
And then do something.

Her sister-in-law helped her in this effort,
To take the right step, the father guided,
Past is past,
Start a new chapter, as you have decided.

In father's talk, she now found happiness,
She listened to his suggestions,
Started doing meditation,
And hoped for better conditions.

*****

- ***MANY TESTING SITUATIONS WILL TEST YOU. NEVER LOSE WITHIN.***
- ***YOU MAY NOT ALWAYS BE A WINNER.***
- ***THINK, ANALYSE AND BE WITH HIM. BECOME SELF-RELIANT.***

*****

Life says, keep on moving,
Stopping means accepting a defeat,
Life offers many ways,
Advising us never to retreat.

In difficulty, others may be helpful,
May try their best to make you cheerful,
But, the best help can come from within,
As the most sincere and strongest friend lies within.

He may let you know the ways,
Getting your jobs done, will provide you peace,
Making you comfortable in your thoughts,
Will put you in ease.

Will provide you contentment,
Will teach you, what is detachment?
Will make you dutiful,
Will heal your wounds and make you blissful.

In the hope of meeting her husband,
The time started to fly,
She was studying and dreaming,
To make a good family, she would try.

Her mother spoke very less,
She was mostly found on bed,
She had stopped going to the parties,
It looked that all her desires to fly, had gone dead.

Her daughter-in-law, she had not yet fully accepted,
Something, she was always thinking and thinking,
Many a times, her husband tried to discuss with her,
But with almost everyone, she had stopped talking.

In difficult times, one has to accept the situation,
One has to prepare, oneself to face,
Mornings do come back,
Human life is a never-ending race.

The mind keeps on running,
The desires, it keeps on creating,
It depends on your state of mind,
In problems, how your body starts acting or reacting.

It is the mind that has to be controlled,
It is the mind that has to be consoled,
It is the mind that gives the courage to fight,
And it is the mind, which in difficulty also, may give delight.

The mind can create the problems,
The mind can solve those problems,
The mind is behind the hatred,
The mind is behind the love.

The earlier we win over the mind,
The earlier we can adjust to the current conditions,
The earlier we mend our mind,
The earlier we will be in a position to face the situations.

As per the father's advice,
Her mind, the girl was able to mend,
Her mother was still struggling,
As she was not prepared to give her thoughts, a bend.

The boy's parents could not know, where the boy is?
They were very tense and worried,
With the boy, they were deeply attached,
With each other, they quarreled.

*****

- ***YOUR REAL PERSONALITY IS THE IMAGE OF YOUR MIND.***
- ***YOUR BODY WILL DO WHAT YOUR MIND DECIDES TO DO.***
- ***DISCIPLINE YOUR MIND AND BUILD A POSITIVE PERSONALITY.***

*****

They had only one son,
On him, all their thoughts were focused,
Earning money was very dear to them,
It was only son and money, they possessed.

They couldn't make their son a good human being,
Those values, they were unaware,
Now, in trouble,
They would get help from where?

In such situations, one may think, whom to consult,
Whom to talk to?
If deeply attached to Him, you would consult Him,
And ask Him, what to do?

For He is the best instructor,
He is the best protector,
Without Him, you are flying and hanging in air,
Low consciousness, and not aware.

With the girl and her parents, they were very much annoyed,
Tension and stress they could not avoid,
The father fell seriously ill,
To control his mind, he had no skill.

He was admitted to a hospital,
With pain, the mother was also suffering,
She felt all the problems were due to the girl,
She was mostly seen grumbling.

Things were getting from bad to worse,
They didn't know what to do?
The business also suffered,
About the son, no one gave any clue.

It was after about six months, a letter dropped in their house,
"I am working as well as studying,
I am somehow earning,
I will be back after studying."

Days and months passed,
On the one hand, the girl waited,
And on the other, the parents,
The girl got a job and was elated.

It was the husband's letters, that infused life in her,
Was also because of family members love and encouragement,
The lessons of hope and patience taught by the father,
Brought the girl out of disappointment.

The boy finally came back,
Both the brothers helped the boy to settle,
The boy had changed a lot in his attitude,
Alone, he was prepared to take on the life's battle.

After some days, he got a good job,
Now, both were earning,
They took a house on rent,
And started a new life from the beginning.

The boy's parents couldn't change their thinking,
Their mind, they couldn't mend,
They couldn't accept the girl,
For pride and anger, a lonely life, they were prepared to spend.

He used to meet his parents,
He would spend time, but never felt at ease,
He was prepared to take care of them,
But, in that environment, now, he never found peace.

*****

- ***THE POWER TO CONTROL THE EMOTIONS IS MORE IMPORTANT THAN THE PHYSICAL AND MONEY POWER.***
- ***AS PER THE LAW OF NATURE, IF YOU DO BAD, YOU WILL RECEIVE BAD, IN THE SAME BIRTH OR FUTURE BIRTHS.***
- ***YOU ARE, THEREFORE, THE MAKER OF YOUR OWN DESTINY.***

*****

**It was six in the morning,
I was enjoying the garden and its greenery,
The sun had shown its color,
The flowers, the fragrance, the breeze, it was a divine scenery.**

**The flowers told me not to go,
The breeze told me to wait,
But, my mind said something to me,
My watch showed me the time and date.**

**My five senses told me to remain there,
My mind reminded me of my duty, to go somewhere,
Why not with the senses, I stay,
Let the time go away.**

**Thought I, had I to live on senses,
I would have lived my life here,
But, the control room at my brain,
My mind was giving an alarm, be aware.**

**The birds came in between,
They further changed the scene,
Their song of caw, tu, so and ho,
Told me not to go.**

**It was then seven,
I never wanted to leave that heaven,
If the whole life could be like this,
This beautiful nature of His.**

But, the reality is different,
I can't have, all the time, my wish,
In a minute, I will be back home,
I may have before me a bitter dish.

I said to me, the five senses, hear, see, touch, taste and smell,
I must control, they will make my life a hell,
The problems may swell,
I have to attend to my mind's intellect, when it starts ringing the bell.